TALKING
— and —
Your Child

A PARENTS' HANDBOOK

CLARE SHAW

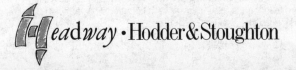

Headway · Hodder & Stoughton

The Publishers would like to thank the children of Charlbury Primary School, Oxfordshire, for their help with the covers for this series.

British Library Cataloguing in Publication Data

Shaw, Clare
  Talking and Your Child. – (Positive
  Parenting Series)
  I. Title   II. Series
  401

  ISBN 0 340 57526 3

First published 1993
Impression number   10 9 8 7 6 5 4 3
Year   1999 1998 1997 1996 1995

Typeset by Rowland Phototypesetting Limited, Bury St Edmunds, Suffolk.
Printed in Great Britain for Hodder & Stoughton Educational, a division of Hodder Headline Plc, 338 Euston Road, London NW1 3BH by Cox & Wyman Ltd, Reading, Berkshire.

Positive Parenting

Positive Parenting is a series of handbooks primarily written for parents, in a clear, accessible style, giving practical information, sound advice and sources of specialist and general help. Based on the authors' extensive professional and personal experience, they cover a wide range of topics and provide an invaluable source of encouragement and information to all who are involved in child care in the home and in the community.

Other books in this series include:

Your child with special needs by Susan Kerr – a guide for the parents of the one-in-five children with special needs, giving families practical advice and emotional support, based on the shared experiences of other parents.

Your child from 5–11 by Jennie and Lance Lindon – a guide showing parents how they can help their children through these crucial early years, stressing the contribution a caring family can make to the emotional, physical and intellectual development of the child.

Help your child through school by Jennie and Lance Lindon – a guide which looks at the school years from the perspective of the family, showing how parents can help their children to get the most out of their years at primary school and how to ease the transition into secondary education.

Help your child with maths by Sue Atkinson – a comprehensive guide to show parents how they can help develop their children's mathematical awareness and confidence from babyhood through the primary years and into secondary school.

Help your child with reading and writing by Lesley Clark – a guide which describes the stages children go through when learning to read and write and shows parents how they can encourage and enjoy their children's early development in these vital areas.

Help your child with a foreign language by Opal Dunn – written for all parents, including those who do not speak a foreign language, this guide examines the right time to start teaching a child a foreign language, how to begin, and how to progress to fluency.

Prepare your child for school by Clare Shaw – a very practical guide for parents whose children are about to start school.

Teenagers in the family by Debi Roker and John Coleman of the Trust for the Study of Adolescence covers all the major issues that parents face as their children pass through the turbulent teenage years, such as rules and regulations, setting boundaries, communication, decision-making, risky behaviour, health, and problems at school.

Teenagers and sexuality by Debi Roker and John Coleman of the Trust for Adolescence gives practical advice for parents who are finding it difficult to talk to their teenagers about sex and who need help to understand, and deal with, their teenagers' emerging sexuality.

Contents

CHAPTER ONE

Talk: What's it all about?

It's a wonderful moment when your child first babbles at you and you suddenly lose all those inhibitions and find yourself making noises back at her. It's also really magical when she says her first words. It doesn't stop there either – you will have many years of listening to your child say the most delightful, amusing, sweet, embarrassing, aggravating (but always clever) things. Learning to talk is one of the most fascinating and important aspects of a child's development. No wonder so many parents want to know how to help their children with communication, realising that their role is so important in its development. However, learning to talk doesn't always go according to plan and there may be worrying times when a child doesn't seem to be talking as well as her contemporaries. He may be slow starting, reluctant to speak to anyone outside the family or seem to have a particular problem with the sounds of speech. Some parents even worry about their child talking too much! Whatever the cause for concern, parents and anyone else dealing with children want to know when these little problems really *are* problems or when they are just normal stages of development.

Put a child in an environment where she hears other people talking and she will learn to talk adequately. Put her in an environment with adults who emphasise communication skills in the family, who stimulate this area of development from an early age and who really listen to their child and she will learn to talk early and well. Obviously parents with this knowledge are keen to know exactly *how* to stimulate talking in the most effective and enjoyable way.

What is talk?

There is more to the development of communication than your child learning to say words. Communication is a two-way process involving listening and understanding as well as talking. The talking element of the communication involves saying the sounds of speech correctly, using the sounds in words and putting these words into sentences. There is also a non-verbal aspect of communication which includes body language and gesture. This can tell us just as much about what someone is trying to say as the words themselves. There are many words used to describe these aspects of communication and it can be very confusing. The following definitions should make things a little clearer:

Articulation   This refers to the way we say the individual sounds of speech – *sh*, *p*, *k* and so on. If a child has difficulty saying the sounds, she is said to have a problem with articulation.

Speech   This also refers to the sounds we use when we talk.

Language   This goes beyond the way we form individual sounds to look at words and sentences – how they are used *and* understood. English, French, German etc. are languages but 'language' refers to the way we put our thoughts and ideas into words.

Expressive language   The words and sentences we say. If a child has a problem with expressive language, it probably means that he is not able to use words in the way we would expect from a child of his age. We would describe the expressive language of, say, a two-year-old as just beginning to put words together with a vocabulary of more than fifty words.

Language comprehension   This refers to the language we understand. A child has good language comprehension if she can understand the words and sentences she hears other people saying.

Vocabulary The words that a child uses. A child with a good vocabulary knows and uses a wide variety of individual words.

Grammar The rules of putting words together into sentences including using past and future tenses, word endings and so on.

Who is interested in talk?

Anybody who works with or has their own children is interested in the way they talk and the way they learn to talk. After all, talking not only allows children to express their needs but it expresses their personality and helps them to build up relationships with other people.

Parents A good understanding of speech and language development helps parents to understand their child's abilities and limitations at each stage. An essential part of parenting has to be to help each child develop. Parents are the most important people to help a child talk.

Health visitors One of the most important aspects of a health visitor's role is to prevent problems and to spot any which might occur. A health visitor therefore keeps a close eye on each child as he or she develops to make sure all is going well. This will involve carrying out regular developmental checks which will necessarily involve checking speech and language. Checks at around two and three years are probably the most crucial and if the health visitor feels your child is not talking or understanding language in an appropriate way for her age, she will refer her to a speech and language therapist. Similarly, if you have any worries about your child, you can call your health visitor to discuss it further.

Playgroup leaders and nursery school teachers The purpose of pre-school education is to give your child the right experiences to enhance his development and social skills and to prepare him for school. Nursery workers are therefore keen to incorporate communication skills into the daily routine. Children will be encouraged to talk and cooperate with each other, they will be encouraged to give their 'news' in an informal group chat and will, of course, be given the opportunity to listen to stories and join in with songs and rhymes. Nursery teachers and playgroup leaders will help shy children who are reluctant to talk and should spot any problems with language development.

Teachers Speech and language development does not stop when your child starts school. Teachers will be particularly interested in the way your child uses her communication skills, and she will be encouraged to talk to other children as well as the teacher. Again, news time or informal discussions will be part of daily school life. Later, teachers will help children to use language imaginatively and creatively both in speaking and writing.

Doctors If you have any worries about your child's language development your GP will refer you to a speech and language therapist. You should see him straight away if you are at all concerned about your child's hearing as this will obviously affect his ability to learn to talk.

When are we interested in talk?

Talking doesn't start when your child says her first words and end once she is able to have little conversations with you. In fact, your child is learning about talking from the moment you look at your brand new baby and say 'Hello, welcome to the world.' And she is communicating from the moment you hear her very first cry. Talking continues to develop over many years and it is difficult to say exactly when the process of language learning is complete but it continues to develop at least until the end of the primary school years. So talk to your child from day one and don't ever feel that your role in encouraging good communication is over.

TALK: WHAT'S IT ALL ABOUT?

Why is talking so important?

Your child will have built up a close relationship with you well before she starts to talk and she will communicate with you long before she can actually say words. However, many parents find that the relationship with their child really takes off once they can talk together. Your child's personality will certainly be reflected in the way she talks and the things she says and perhaps it is these first words and little sentences which seem to turn your baby into a little person.

We all look forward to our child's first words and listen with pride when she says something clever or amusing. First words are, in many ways, more exciting than those first steps or the first tooth. This may be because we know that talking is a stepping stone to so many other things. Language gives a child a key to learning and finding out about the world. Parents are also aware that their child has learnt to talk from listening to them. It is therefore a particularly proud time when a child starts talking because parents know that they have 'taught' their child to speak and can take at least some of the credit for her achievements.

Parent-traps

Having established that parents are the most important people involved in the process of a child learning to talk, it is worth pointing out a few traps that parents can fall into during these critical years.

- If your child speaks well, give yourself a pat on the back. However, it doesn't always follow that if your child has problems or is slow starting off, it is all your fault. There are many other factors involved so never blame yourself or your partner.
- The milestones given for when children are likely to say their first words, use short sentences etc. are only rough guides. The ages given for achieving a certain level of language are very variable indeed, so if your child is not using words by the

so-called 'average' time, then don't panic. Try not to compare your child with the average ages given here or in any other book unless your child is obviously a long way behind. Each child is an individual and develops at his or her own pace.

- Helping your child to talk should be an enjoyable experience for both of you. Putting pressure on her does not help, in fact it can have the adverse effect. Keep talking fun!

- Avoid pointless questions or demands such as 'What's that?' or 'Say ambulance' and so on. A natural two-way communication between you and your child is more beneficial and much more enjoyable.

- If your child is later starting to talk than a friend of the same age, it doesn't mean he is less intelligent. Try not to compare your child with others – easier than it sounds – just enjoy his development as it happens.

- Talking to children comes naturally to some parents but by no means all. If you find it hard to know exactly what to say to your two-year-old or if you find babbling to your baby nothing more than embarrassing, give yourself time. Parenting is a skill and practice makes perfect.

Talk-time tips

- Take time to listen to your child at all stages of her development. Record her talking and you will notice far more when you listen again carefully. Record your child every six months, remembering to say the date into the tape-recorder after each sample. If, at any time, you feel your child is not making much progress, listen to the previous recordings and you will certainly notice a world of difference.

- Listen to yourself talking to your child on these recordings. Make sure that what you say is meaningful and interesting to your child. Over a period of time, you

TALK: WHAT'S IT ALL ABOUT?

will notice that the way you speak to your child changes as she matures and is able to take in and understand more of what you say.

- Have fun and enjoy your child's development. Make a note of all the funny things he says – you'll both enjoy looking back on them in years to come.

CHAPTER TWO

Baby noises
(the first year)

Babies communicate from the moment they are born, crying to tell the world that they are hungry, hot, uncomfortable or perhaps just in need of a cuddle. Even that very first cry at birth seems to be telling us something – perhaps 'Help!' 'Please look after me' or even 'I've arrived – do something!' The new baby immediately gets a response from her mother and the very first communication has begun.

Babies are born understanding nothing of what we say and only have the ability to communicate through crying. Yet, after just one year, your baby will have made incredible progress. He will be using, or on the verge of using, words, he will be communicating his needs through gesture or just the expression on his face and he will have started to make sense of some of the words and sentences he is bombarded with from other people. Most important of all, he will have discovered the joy of communication and will be dying to take an active part in the conversation he hears around him.

All about crying

Perhaps if your baby could tap you on the shoulder and say 'Excuse me Mummy/Daddy but my nappy's full and I'm awfully hungry', then crying would not be quite so necessary. But for the moment, crying is your baby's main means of communicating her needs. A cry can say 'I'm tired', 'I'm hungry', 'I'm thirsty', 'I have a pain', 'I'm bored', 'I'm lonely', 'I'm wet', 'I'm afraid' and so on. All these reasons for crying suggest that she has a particular need which can be met by you. And if you don't respond to that need then crying will continue, communicating her frustration. In the early stages a lot of guesswork may be needed in order to interpret exactly what your baby is trying to tell you, and that guesswork will largely depend on the circumstances – when she was last fed or changed, when she last had a sleep or whether she has just had a quick and hurried feed. Interpreting the cry will continue even after you have responded to it – Does she stop crying when you pick her up, feed her or rock her to sleep for example?

As the days and weeks go by, it has been found that many mothers start to respond to the particular cry that they hear their babies make, so that when their baby cries, they are more likely to interpret it correctly the first time and make the appropriate response.

Your baby's cry in the early weeks is really just a reflex action. He is not able to reason that if he cries then you will know that he is hungry and do something about it. If he is hungry then he will cry automatically. Later, crying will become more intentional so that when your baby sees his juice and wants it, he will cry to make you get it for him. This reasoned, intentional type of cry happens after several months of life. However, you will respond to both sorts of cry in much the same way – your baby needs something and you will do your best to provide it. In this way, your baby very soon learns that communication gets things done and the desire to communicate and ultimately to talk has begun.

The language of cry babies

Wolff, a psychologist, describes four different types of cries which mothers in his experiments were able to identify:

1 The hunger cry, sometimes used in discomfort: A rhythmic

sound with half a second of crying alternating with half a second of breathing in.

2 The pain cry: Relatively long bursts of crying lasting for about four seconds at a time.

3 The 'mad' cry used in frustration: Similar pattern to the hunger cry but more noise, especially from the throat. The hunger cry is more open.

4 The 'fake' cry or cry for attention: A low-pitched moan with occasional sudden jumps to a higher pitch.

However, you cannot really learn the theory of what the different types of cries mean. You have to get to know *your* baby and learn what *she* is telling *you*.

At a glance: What your six-month-old can do

Half-way through his first year, and what can your baby do now? You will probably be proud of the way he has started to sit up, drink from his beaker, shake his rattle or throw his soft ball. But what about his communication skills? Before you next say 'Of course, he isn't really talking yet . . .', think about the following skills he has already acquired:

- She will watch your face while you talk, then babble or coo back to you and listen to your reply when she's finished. She already knows that a conversation means taking turns.
- He can follow the rhythmic patterns of your speech. Watch carefully and you will often see him move his arms and legs in unison.
- She will understand the different tones of your voice. Your soothing voice reassures her, your sing-song chatter excites her.
- He can make a variety of speech sounds and can practise

moving his lips about. He will even try to copy your
facial movements.
- She can let you know exactly what she wants. She
communicates her needs effectively whether it's with a
scream, a reach out or just a gaze in the right direction.

'Goo – goo' and 'ga–ga' – playing with sounds

During the first few weeks your baby will cry when she's distressed
or in need of something, but very few sounds of contentment will
be heard. It's not that your baby is unhappy but more often than
not, when your baby is content, she's fast asleep. However, from
about six weeks your baby will not only be able to communicate
her needs but will be able to communicate pleasure and contentment by means of gurgling and cooing sounds. Cooing takes the
form of open vowel sounds – 'oooh', 'ahhh' and so on – and is
often accompanied by excited movements of the arms and legs.
Some gurgling and guttural sounds from the back of the throat may
be heard but 'hard' sounds made with the lips and tongue are not
usually present.

By five or six months, your baby will begin to make a much
greater variety of sounds. You will now hear those hard consonant
sounds made with the lips and tongue – 'goo', 'adah', 'ma' etc.
This is the start of the delightful stage of babbling.

Babbling will start off as short single syllable utterances – 'ma',
'da', 'goo' etc. – but shortly after this the repertoire of sounds continues to expand and double syllables – 'dada', 'gara', 'aroo' – are
used. By about eight months, longer strings of babble will be made,
some of which will sound remarkably like words! In fact, because
sounds made at the front of the mouth tend to predominate to begin
with, 'mama' and 'dada' are very likely to be heard and it's tempting
to interpret them as real words.

TALKING AND YOUR CHILD

Your baby will not only babble in response to you talking directly to him but will babble when he's alone. This may be in his cot when he wakes up or when he's involved in playing with his toys or perhaps when he's lying on the rug having a kick. Playing with sounds like this is an important step towards learning the sounds of speech he will need later.

In fact, to begin with, the babble of babies will sound very similar whatever the nationality of the baby. If you were to listen to a Russian or Icelandic child in the first stages of babbling then you would not be able to distinguish her from a British baby. The same sorts of sounds are heard in all babies, some of which they will need for speaking their language and some of which they won't. However, when much longer strings of babble occur at around eight or nine months, gradually the sounds of the child's native language predominate and differences from country to country will be heard.

Rubbish talk and copycats

By about nine months, babies start to use long strings of babble known as jargon. Jargon sounds very much like 'real' talking when heard from a distance because it reflects the up and down intonation patterns and rhythms of real adult speech. When your baby strings sounds together in a pattern which rises to a higher note at the end of the sentence, you will feel sure that she has asked you an important question. Jargon contains many of the sounds of speech which your child will need later on and will begin to sound more and more like a nonsense style of English.

Most parents reinforce those strings of sounds which most resemble real words, giving their children lots of smiles and chat when they hear 'mama' and 'dada' or anything else which could be a word. It's possible that this reinforcement makes these strings of sounds more likely to occur. But they are not really words until they are used meaningfully to label a person or object – at this stage your baby is still playing with sounds.

As with babbling, your baby will use jargon to chat to you and also to entertain himself when he's playing in his cot. At this stage, your baby will enjoy copying noises and sounds that you make such as coughing or blowing raspberries. Even after those first words appear, jargon will continue – sometimes interspersed with those new words your child has learnt.

Baby-body language

Body language refers to all those things we do, apart from actually talking, which tell other people something. Smiling, the way we stand, how we move – they all communicate some message. Babies soon learn how to tune into our body language and we, too, can learn to tune into theirs.

A new baby can soon communicate with body language. She shows us she likes faces by fixing her gaze on us. She turns her head away when bored or perhaps over-awed by too much stimulation. Her body will be relaxed and floppy when tired, stiff and tense when needing to fill her nappy. And we all recognise that contented look after a feed. Added to this, babies are born with an in-built piece of body language. It's a well known fact that we naturally find dilated or large pupils in the eyes very attractive; and all babies have them.

The most important expression to most parents is the smile. This comes after six weeks or so of hard slog day and night. Suddenly he smiles and it's all worthwhile. A baby often smiles first in response to looking at someone special to him. It means 'I'm happy' and 'I love you' and it knocks you out. Babies often have their own greeting, saying 'Hello' to you with excited kicking of their arms and legs.

After only two or three months, a baby will communicate many emotions through her facial expressions – excitement, distress, pleasure, pain, curiosity, boredom, tiredness and contentment to name but a few. At three months a baby will begin to kick her legs and arms in response to a familiar sound, such as her mother approaching or the bath water running. Her excitement is easy to interpret. At six months old, he will look towards and often reach for toys and objects he wants. An accompanying cry makes his message all too obvious. By seven or eight months, babies have a very different posture when sitting on a parent's knee compared with sitting on a stranger's knee. You can tell who they feel most comfortable with – a rigid more upright posture means they are not completely at ease. By nine months, a baby begins to point towards things. She may also hold out her arms to be picked up. By the end of the year, she will be copying most of our gestures such as clapping with pleasure and waving goodbye.

What babies understand

Right from the beginning, your child will understand more than she is able to say and this pattern continues as her language develops.

Your baby will take notice of all interesting sounds but will have a particular inborn interest in human voices. After only a few weeks, he will recognise your voice. In fact, some research suggests that babies can hear their mother's voice in the womb, and after birth the recognition is almost instant. Your baby will soon begin to understand and respond to your body language, particularly your smile which he will love. By four months, he will be able to sort out what tone of voice you are talking in, being soothed by your quiet, sympathetic voice, excited by your laughter and frightened by any loud angry voice.

By six or seven months, your baby will understand that speech is for communication. She will often watch adults intently as they talk to one another, turning her head from speaker to speaker and appearing to listen to every word. By nine months, your baby will begin to understand individual words such as 'no' and 'bye-bye', responding with an appropriate action or gesture. She will also understand many of our everyday gestures such as shaking a disapproving finger or waving.

By the end of this first year, your child will have a good understanding of what language is all about and will be beginning to understand names for some familiar objects and people. Soon he will be ready to join in with his own words.

How to talk to your baby

Eye contact is very important and you will find that your baby will naturally look into your eyes. If she turns away, she's probably tired or has had enough for the time being. Your baby may have a 'peak' time for talking, becoming particularly chatty in the bath, lying on her mat or perhaps kicking in the cot first thing in the morning. Allow an extra five minutes or so at her chatty time of the day and enjoy a good conversation.

Copy your baby's noises and make some new ones back to him. But talk to him in sentences as well – he will respond to the up and down pattern of speech which he will imitate from about nine months. Allow your baby to get a word in edgeways. Communication is a two-way process, so when you've said your bit, stop and listen to your baby's 'reply' – giving her plenty of time to make a response. Also, don't always start up a conversation when your baby is wrapped in blankets. Babies 'talk' with their whole bodies and the leg and arm movements are communicating to you as well.

From about seven or eight months, concentrate on talking about what you're doing there and then. Your baby won't respond to the past or future but will soon pick up the meanings of words which are used in context. At the end of the year, start to emphasise the names of familiar objects repeating the word many times – 'Here's your *drink*', would you like your *drink* now? I'll put your *drink* on the table then.'

Games and activities

Round and round the garden

Play this and other repetitive games such as 'This little piggy', 'Peek-a-boo' and 'Ring a ring of roses'. There is little need to describe these familiar games, and it is indeed their familiarity and repetition which babies adore. Your baby will giggle and vocalise in anticipation of the repeated actions and as she begins to use words, you can leave the last one off for her to say – 'Like a teddy ____', 'We all fall ____' etc.

Mirror, mirror

Sit next to your child in front of the mirror and make faces and noises together. Hang a baby mirror in his cot and he will chat to himself as he goes to sleep or wakes up.

Who said that?

Use a tape-recorder to record your baby's babbling and play it back to her. You could try making farm animal noises together, perhaps with the help of toys or a picture book, and then listen to yourselves.

Shopping baskets

As your child approaches his first birthday, you will find that she loves to put toys and objects in and out of various containers. Sit down together at a quiet time and fill up your baskets or boxes with familiar things, talking about them as you do so. Emphasise the key words and when your child is ready, see if he can find the right toy when you ask for it.

Puppets

Puppets can be made simply out of old socks or paper bags. All babies love smiling faces and will be attracted by their movement and the accompanying funny voices provided by you. This should get your baby babbling.

Questions ... questions ... questions ...

(*I'm a busy mum with several older children. I just can't set aside part of the day for talking to the youngest. Will my baby miss out?*)

Talking is not a separate activity – conversations can take place when you're busy doing other things, whether it's changing a nappy or feeding your baby. Every time you're with your baby, you are probably communicating with her and she will also benefit from communicating with a variety of other people including older brothers and sisters. Everybody looks different and talks in a different way and your baby can't fail to be stimulated by all this. She will also enjoy listening to all the conversations going on around her – a busy household is rarely a quiet one. Don't feel you need to set aside a long period for talking – babies have limited concentration and the five minutes it takes to change a nappy is a long time when you're only four months old.

(*I feel embarrassed about talking to my baby – it doesn't really feel natural to me and it's even worse when I know that someone is listening.*)

Many parents feel foolish to start with especially as the conversation may seem a bit one-sided. But it does become easier with time, especially once your baby starts making noises back at you. If you find baby talk and making silly noises embarrassing, then just start by talking to your baby as you would to anyone else – there's no need to do a special voice. Try to find a time when you can shut the bedroom door (remembering to turn the baby-intercom off) and have a long chat without anyone interrupting you. Soon you'll be doing it in the most public of places and you'll find that nobody thinks you're in the slightest bit odd. In fact it would be odd *not* to talk to your baby.

> (*How would I know if my young baby was deaf?*
> *She doesn't always take much notice of the*
> *noises around her.*)

Health visitors normally carry out routine hearing checks at around eight months. This age is not chosen at random – this is when babies will most reliably turn round to see what is making a new and interesting sound slightly behind them at ear level. The noise must be interesting to get a response. You will find that your baby won't take much notice of a continuous and familiar noise, particularly if she is engrossed in something. It's easy to think that there may be a problem because your baby takes no notice of a drum that's being banged for the umpteenth time when she is having more fun playing with her bricks – her lack of interest does not necessarily mean that she has a hearing problem.

A profoundly deaf child is usually identified, often by a parent, very early on. She may not startle to a sudden noise or freeze in response to a new continuous sound. She may also be startled by your sudden appearance next to the cot even after the usual noises of entering a room. Later, deaf babies babble in the usual way up to about seven months or so but the more sing-song babble (jargon) will not appear and eventually the babble may stop altogether.

Some babies may suffer from a temporary hearing loss caused by frequent ear infections. If this is identified and treated promptly then any delay in learning sounds will be put right very quickly. So if you are in any doubt, discuss this with your health visitor.

> (*Does eating have anything to do with speech? My*
> *baby seems to be making even more sounds*
> *now that he has started to chew properly.*)

Learning to eat properly is important for developing intelligible speech. Even the newborn baby has to form a strong seal with his lips for sucking, which will be needed later for making sounds such as 'p', 'b' and 'm'. Eating and speech skills develop alongside each other so that a baby who merely sucks will just use open vowel cooing sounds such as 'ooh' and 'aah'. A six-month-old on solids and chewing the occasional rusk will be babbling with a much wider variety of sounds. Giving your baby occasional rusks or slices of fruit to chew on will exercise those parts of the mouth needed for talking.

Children who have problems with feeding and chewing sometimes go on to develop speech problems, but remember that learning to chew and self-feed is a gradual process and a messy stage is perfectly normal.

> *I talk to my baby continuously, shaking rattles and playing her nursery rhyme tape in the background. She often turns her head away or even cries – is she bored?*

Quite the opposite. A baby can be over-stimulated especially when she is still very young. Having all her senses bombarded at once with too much to look at and hear can be too much to cope with, even frightening. Your baby will naturally love the sound of your voice, looking into your eyes and eventually learning to join in. This is enough for her at any one time – she won't want or need other noises or moving toys to distract her. So take the lead from your baby and give her as much or as little stimulation as she can cope with and enjoy. If she turns away or cries, take a good look at what you're doing.

As your baby develops, you will find that she takes to things that are new but not too new. In other words she may enjoy the familiar game of Round and round the garden but once she's had enough, will still enjoy the same game but done by someone else with a different voice, such as Dad.

> *What's the best way to get my one-year-old to say words? He won't repeat them after me and just wants to play instead.*

TALKING AND YOUR CHILD

You can't make a baby say words – he'll speak as soon as he's ready and trying to force words out will only serve to put him off. Even once he has mastered a few words, he will use them as and when he likes and asking him to repeat them is not the best form of encouragement. Instead, create the opportunity for him to use them, perhaps through play or looking at books. You can also give him choices – 'Do you want orange or Ribena?' or 'Do you want to take Piggy or Teddy to bed?' This not only gives him the opportunity of using the words he knows, but shows him how useful these words can be.

Don't think of playing as totally unrelated to learning to talk. Remember that words are symbols which represent objects or ideas. For example, the word 'house' is used to represent the building we live in. Toys and pictures are symbols too – a doll represents a person for example. So when your child plays, not only is he chatting and learning names for things, but he is learning about symbols, and children need to be able to play with these symbolic toys (miniatures of the real thing) before they start to use words.

CHAPTER THREE

First words
(one to two years)

One of the most exciting times of your child's development is when she starts using words and this will happen roughly between eleven and sixteen months, although the age is very variable. It is not always easy to pinpoint the exact time when that first word is used, as your baby's jargon will resemble words so closely that you can never be entirely sure what is or isn't a word. Some parents suddenly realise that their child has been using a particular word for some time but perhaps because the word was not pronounced all that clearly (which is common and normal at this age) they hadn't been aware of what she was saying. On the other hand, some parents are sure that their child is saying all sorts of words when in fact they just think that they can hear them amongst their child's babble when she's playing with sounds. However, once your child has three or four words in her vocabulary you will be absolutely sure and no doubt hope that she'll perform them in the company of all your friends and relatives so they will see just how clever she is.

To begin with, you may find that the jargon – or play with sounds – continues, although it will be interspersed with the new words. However, the new words will be used mainly on their own and usually to communicate to other people, while the jargon will become more or less confined to when your child is playing or talking to himself. Soon you will find that your child is repeating words after you and echoing the last word of your sentence. You may not always realise that he was even listening to you – so now's the time to be careful what you're saying and avoid using any words you definitely don't want repeated!

Your child's vocabulary will gradually increase over the year so that by the time she is two years old, she will be able to say at least fifty words. Around that time, there tends to be a sudden spurt in vocabulary often accompanied by constant repetition of the phrase 'What's that?' Suddenly you will find that barely a day goes by without your child saying a word you haven't heard from her before and you will stop counting.

To begin with, your child may use a word in a wider sense than we would. This is called 'over-generalisation' and you will find that the word 'Daddy' refers to all men and the word 'dog' to all four-legged animals and so on. This seems to occur while your child is sorting out the exact meaning of all these words and also before he has enough words to correctly name all the animals, for example, without having to use the one word he does know. So as his vocabulary increases, this trend will stop and he will no longer be referring to the milkman as 'Daddy' or be calling your neighbour's prize poodle a 'cow'. In the same way, your child will over-restrict a word so that perhaps when he uses the word 'teddy' it only refers to his and not to any other. Or perhaps the word 'dog' to him means just the one you have at home, whereas all others are ignored or called cats.

What is a word?

Why is it that when your child is playing in her cot one morning and is quite clearly saying 'dada' over and over again, this does not count as a real word? Yet when she greets her father a few weeks later with exactly the same string of sounds – 'dada' – this quite clearly *is* a word? Perhaps the following definitions of a word will help you to decide whether your child is well and truly talking.

- A word is used to label or make a comment about something. Pointing to Mummy or saying hello to Mummy with the word 'mama' is fine. Making the same string of sounds by accident and not in any connection with Mummy is not using a word.
- The word must be used consistently if it really is a word. If teddy is referred to by a different combination of sounds every time, perhaps your child has not really got a word for teddy even though it once sounded remarkably similar.
- A word does not have to sound exactly like we would say it. If your child says 'poo' every time she sees a spoon, then this certainly counts as a word.
- Your child may not use the same word as we would – 'moo' is a perfectly acceptable word for cow, to start with.
- Your child's word may not have exactly the right meaning – perhaps he calls the Christmas tree a 'pretty' because this is the word he has heard in association with it. In this case the word 'pretty' actually means Christmas tree and is only used as such. It is nevertheless still a word.
- Your child may appear to be using two or three words together when in fact, for her it is only one word. 'Allgone', for example, may always be used together as one word even though we would normally think of it as two. Many children pick up our phrase 'Here you are' when we give them something. This comes out as a sort of 'Eeyore' and really means 'give'. This can also be thought of as one word.

Apples before alligators: which words first?

First words are nearly always those which are most important to a child. Of course, there will be enormous variations between children, depending on their different circumstances but it's still surprising how often some of the same words come up when parents are asked what their child's first words were. Although most first words are names and labels for things, sometimes social words such as 'bye-bye' are amongst the first. First words so often fall into the following categories:

- Names of toys or important objects in the child's routine.
- Food.
- Animals.
- Names of favourite people.
- Clothes.
- Transport.

Within these categories, some words are more likely to occur than others:

- Words for things the child can actually use are more common than larger items – so 'key' comes before 'house' and 'socks' before 'dungarees'.
- Some words are particularly useful for getting things done - the words 'cup' or 'drink' for example – and they are likely to come fairly easily.
- Specific labels come before more general ones so that the word 'penny' will be used before 'coin, 'chair' comes before 'furniture' and 'dog' before 'animal'.
- However, very specialised words are not heard early. The word 'fish', for example, is sufficient for your child to tell us what is on her plate. There's no need for her to go into whether it's cod or haddock.

After your child has a few words to use as labels, the following types of words may appear:

- Action words – 'up', 'down', 'give' etc.
- Social words – 'please', 'thank you' and particularly 'no'.
- Some descriptive words – 'red', 'dirty'.
- Some command words, particularly 'more', 'again' and 'mine'!

The following types of words are rarely heard at the first word stage:

- Words about the child's state – so 'eat' will be used rather than 'hungry', and 'sleep' instead of 'tired'.
- Those little words of speech which don't mean much on their own – 'but', 'and', 'if' and so on.

- Position words – 'in', 'on', 'under'.
- Words which represent people such as 'he', 'she' and 'him', although 'me' and 'mine' sometimes occur during the first word stage.
- Most descriptive words – 'long', 'big', 'pretty', 'soft'.

One-word wonders

You may think that while your child can only use one word at a time, she is limited to just labelling the people and items around her. But if you think that all a one-year-old can do is tell you what things are, then think again.

Listen and watch your child carefully and you will soon learn that one word alone can tell you a multitude of different things. When you decipher exactly what your child's word is trying to tell you, you will find yourself responding both to the situation and your child's body language. So, for example, if your child says 'sock' you will look to see if she's got a sock on or if she's playing with her bare-footed dolly before deciding that she is asking for a sock. Similarly, for example, the word 'Daddy' can mean:

'There's Daddy' when pointing, smiling or looking at the man in question.
'Hello Daddy' when greeting him as he comes in from work.
'That belongs to Daddy' when looking at his coat, shoes or whatever.
'I want Daddy' when shouted, screamed or whimpered.
'Is that Daddy?' when said in a rising voice like a question, after hearing the front door slam.
'This is for Daddy' when handing him a half-chewed biscuit.
'A big one' when pointing to the biggest car, teddy or whatever.
'Daddy' and 'baby' are often used as an indicator of size.
'Daddy did that' when looking at the new shelf in the bathroom.

First words are used for:

- Greeting somebody ('hello', 'hi').

- Telling us what something is ('book').
- Asking for something ('drink', 'more').
- Asking if that really is the name of something ('dolly?').
- Giving someone a command ('give').
- Giving self a command ('blow' – e.g. when blowing own nose).
- Denying or refusing something ('no').
- Making a comment about something ('yum', 'wet').
- Practising (e.g. – repeating words over and over to self 'car, car, car').
- Building a relationship with someone ('mummy, kiss, hello').

What one-year-olds can understand

It's so easy to get caught up in the exciting fact that your child can say real words that it can be forgotten that her understanding of language is also developing at a tremendous rate. Children always understand many more words than they can say, so for example, when your child can say twenty words herself, she will be able to understand at least a hundred.

By about fourteen months, your child will not only understand many individual words but will begin to understand and carry out simple instructions such as 'Don't do that', 'Give me that book' and 'Come and get your tea'. He will be able to hand you a familiar object when you ask for it and point to a picture in a book. You will now find yourself having a 'real' conversation with your child. He will be able to understand your simple sentences and reply appropriately even with his limited language. To begin with, your child may be relying a lot on the clues you give him with your body. For example, you may lean forward, pucker your lips and say 'Give Mummy a kiss'. He doesn't need to understand many words to know precisely what you want him to do! Gradually he will learn to pick out the key words in your instruction and then

FIRST WORDS

make sense of the whole sentence. For example, if you point to a chair and say 'Put your coat on there', he only has to understand and key into the word 'coat' to do as you say. He certainly wouldn't need to know the meaning of all five words in your instruction, although your clue of pointing to the chair would have been important.

If your instruction involves understanding more than one important word, then your one-year-old may have problems. If you tell her to put the dolly on the table with no other clues such as pointing, she may key into the word 'table' but put teddy on it or key into 'dolly' but put it on the chair. Clearly, your child is limited by the amount of information she can cope with at a time. At this stage, you would need to hand dolly to your child first and then ask her to put it on the table.

Your child's understanding of what you say to him develops very quickly during this year and by two years, he will be able to understand several hundred words and will respond to those commands involving two key words such as 'Put your book on the bed'.

At a glance: what your eighteen-month-old can do.

There is no such thing as a normal, average eighteen-month-old. Every child is different and will develop at a different rate. But roughly speaking, your child will:

- Use several words spontaneously (i.e. not just repeated after you).
- Copy even more words after you and often echo back the end of your sentence.
- Continue to jargon and play with sounds, chatting to herself.
- Use her words and gestures to ask for things.
- Attempt to sing nursery rhymes along with you.
- Understand most everyday words and names of familiar objects.
- Understand short and simple instructions involving one key word e.g. 'Fetch your *cup*'.

- Play meaningfully with dolls and teddies, brushing their hair, putting them to bed etc.
- Enjoy books, pointing to items when you ask. Eager to know the names of things.
- Understand what talking is all about and use his few words to engage in a proper two-way conversation with a familiar adult.
- Know when a question is addressed to her and immediately respond in some way.

Allgoneaway

If you listen to a tape of an unfamiliar foreign language, you will find that it is extremely difficult to decipher when one word ends and the next one starts. The words just seem to run into each other. Think about how we talk in English – we certainly don't talk by saying each word individually, pausing between each one. We may greet someone, saying 'Hello, Howareyou? Isn'titlovelyweatherfor-thetimeofyear' and they will know perfectly well what we mean. But how on earth do babies and toddlers sort out the individual words? You might say to your child 'Heresacup', yet she soon learns that the plastic item she has her drink in is called a 'cup' and not a 'heresacup'. Occasionally, two words are used together so frequently that your child may use them as one. The classic example is 'allgone'. Some children make very individual 'mistakes' in this way, treating two words as one when using particular phrases. One child not only used 'stop it' as one word but thought it was part of her name. Her mother would frequently say 'Laura – stop it', and when asked her name, Laura once replied 'Laura Stopit.' Another child, Lee, went through a stage of saying 'What's that?' just before his second birthday. His mother would reply 'That's a cup, Lee' or 'That's a car, Lee' and before long, he had a good vocabulary of words including 'cuplee' and 'carlee'.

These examples are, of course, exceptions which is why they are amusing. In most cases, children have no problems sorting out one word from another. There are several reasons for this. For one thing, children of only a few months old listen carefully to the rise and fall pattern of our speech. These natural rhythms and stresses make it easier to single words out. We also tend to emphasise key words when we talk to children and use individual words more often than when we talk to adults. Finally, children are not just wallflowers when it comes to learning language – they don't just stand there and take it all in, they are active participants, practising words and playing with sounds at every opportunity.

The parenting part

Your child will learn words from the people around who talk to her, particularly you. If you were to ignore every noise she made and only spoke to reprimand her, then she probably wouldn't speak at all. Yet put a child in a home with at least one adult who talks to her and language can hardly fail to develop. Your role is to show your child that communication is both enjoyable and rewarding. Enjoyable because you both like chatting together and rewarding because with only a few words, your child can have quite an effect on those around her. Being able to say 'drink' or 'biscuit' brings particular rewards but being able to say 'no' and 'more' may also be rewarding in that suddenly everybody takes note of what your child does or doesn't want.

While making talk so enjoyable, you also have a role in putting on a demonstration of all those useful words. She won't learn the word for a drink if she never hears it, or if she hears it but can't relate it to any particular thing. But if her drink is there, right in front of her eyes and she hears you say the word 'drink', then she will quickly learn its meaning and eventually say it herself.

How to talk to your one-year-old

- Repeat key words two or three times. For example, you might say 'Time for your *bath*, let's run the water into your *bath*, and put duck in the *bath*.'
- Although emphasising names for things is useful, do talk in sentences but keep them short and simple.
- Use repetition from day to day. If you talk about your child's bath one day, try to discuss it the next. This is not difficult – your child has a fairly repetitive routine and the same conversations do crop up frequently.
- Talk about what you are doing at that moment or about the items there in front of you. If you talk about past events or something in the other room or discuss future plans, your child won't have anything to relate your words to.
- When your child says a word, respond to it so that a conversation is started.
- Respond to your child's word by reinforcing it and adding a little bit more. For example, if your child says 'Drink', you might say 'Yes, it's your drink – your drink of orange.'
- Don't forget to let your child get a word in edgeways. When you're said your bit, stop and listen to your child and give her plenty of time to reply.
- What your child says should form the basis of what you say next. If he says 'dog', then the conversation is about dogs or animals. Don't keep changing the subject.
- Look at the conversation from your child's point of view and talk about what is interesting to her.
- What your child says is important – if the meaning is unclear, don't just ignore it, but repeat back what you think he's said in a questioning tone. Use the situation or what your child is looking at to make a good guess.
- Always give your child your full attention when she talks, and look into her eyes frequently during a conversation.

- Remember that talking to your child does come naturally – you will probably find that you emphasise words, keep your sentences short and listen to your child without even thinking about it.

Here is a conversation between a father and his fourteen-month-old child. Even though the child is only using one-word sentences, it is still very much a conversation.

Jess: Book.
Dad: Yes, it's your book. Do you like that one? (Dad has repeated the word and added some more.)
Jess: Book. (Jess has repeated word so perhaps Dad didn't get message.)
Dad: You want me to read it? (Dad tries again.)
Jess: Yes. Read. (Success. The message has got through.)
Dad: Come and sit here then. (Jess goes to Dad understanding the short instruction straight away.)
Oh look here are some horses. (Dad emphasises key word 'horses'.)
Jess: Horses. (Repetition of last word.)
Dad: And who is this?
Jess: Dog. (Jess practises a word she knows.)
Dad: Yes a dog. A big brown dog. (Dad reinforces it and adds more information.)
Jess: Shop. (Jess seems to change the subject.)
Dad: Shop? (Dad questions what she means.)
Jess: Yea. Shop. Dog. (Jess indicates she associates the dog with a shop.)
Dad: Oh yes, we saw Jim's dog in the shop. (Dad makes a guess as to what Jess might mean.)
Jess: Jim. (Repetition of a key word again.)
Dad: Is this like Jim's dog?
Jess: Yes.
Dad: A bit. And what's this?
Jess: Baa.

Dad: That's right – a sheep. It says baa. (Dad doesn't correct Jess' answer – just gives it back to her in the next sentence.)

How the sounds of speech develop

It is quite normal for your child's first words to be unclear with sounds missed out or some of the wrong sounds used. Some children will speak more clearly than others but no child at this stage will be able to say all her words exactly as an adult would. The same sorts of 'mistakes' tend to be found in all children. Luckily, you will 'tune in' to your child's way of talking and will generally have little difficulty understanding what she's saying. Listen out for the following.

Sound harmony   This is when a word is made easier to pronounce by making the consonants (hard sounds) the same as each other. For example the word 'dog' might be pronounced 'gog' or 'dod'. Sometimes, whole syllables are made the same so that 'bottle' might be pronounced 'bobo'.

Leaving out unstressed parts   In longer words, syllables which are unstressed or sound quieter than the rest of the word are left out completely. In this way 'banana' is typically pronounced 'nana' and 'gain' may be said for 'again'.

Leaving out sounds   The sounds at the ends of words or sometimes in the middle of longer words are often left out. So 'duck' may be pronounced 'du' and 'hat' may be pronounced 'ha'.

Using the 'wrong' sound   Vowel sounds (ee, a, oo etc.) rarely pose any problems but the harder sounds of speech, called consonants, take longer to develop. Those made at the front of the mouth, such as *p*, *b*, *t*, *d*, *m* and *n* tend to be used first and are often used in place of those made at the back of the mouth such as *g* and *k*/*c*. In this way 'car' is often pronounced 'tar' and 'go' is often pronounced 'doe'. Longer consonants such as *s*, *sh* and *f* are often replaced by short, hard consonants so 'sun' may be pronounced 'dun' and 'shoe' may be 'do'. Other sounds which are difficult for the child to say, in particular *l*, *th* and *r*, will either be left out altogether or other sounds used in their place.

Groups of sounds made into one sound   Some words start with whole clusters of sounds like <u>sp</u>ring, <u>sp</u>ider or <u>tr</u>ee. These are too difficult for a new talker to get his tongue around so usually one sound is used instead. In this way, 'spider' and 'tree' will be pronounced 'pider' and 'tee'.

Games and activities

Matching toys and pictures

This is a very good activity if your child is just approaching the first word stage. Draw or cut out pictures of her toys or everyday objects, and see if she can put the object on top of the correct picture. To begin with, use pictures which are a good likeness of the objects. Later the picture may be slightly different so, for example, if her cup is red with two handles, draw a blue one with one handle for her to 'match' it with.

Picture lotto

This is rather like bingo with pictures. You will need two large cards each with six pictures on, together with twelve matching pictures on smaller individual cards. To start with, just give your child one of the large cards and then hand him the smaller pictures, one at a time, to match on to it. Once he is able to match the pictures fairly well, then make it into more of a game. You can now each have one of the large cards and spread the smaller ones upside down on the table. Take it in turns to choose a picture and decide whose board it matches on to, remembering to sit next to, rather than opposite your child so that the pictures are not upside down from his point of view. Call out the name of the picture you select and encourage your child to do the same. If you buy a picture lotto game, choose one with pictures of everyday objects to start with. However, you can easily make this game by collecting two free catalogues and sticking the pictures from one on to a large card and the identical pictures from the other on to individual cards. This way, you could start with fewer items, perhaps three or four, and gradually increase the amount on each card. You can, of course, make another game whenever you want to introduce new words.

Hide it

Your one-year-old may be very active and may not be able to concentrate on games and books for very long. Use her boundless energy to practise her first words by playing hiding games around the room or in the garden. Get her to hide two or three toys around the room. Then ask her to find them one at a time. As her language develops, she can ask *you* to find the toys.

Noise tapes

Tape everyday sounds and play them back to your child who can then guess what the noises are. You can draw pictures to match with the sounds and give your child two or three at a time to choose from. Noises to record could include: the dog barking; running water; the telephone ringing; the doorbell or someone knocking; slamming the door; someone clapping; someone whistling; someone playing a familiar musical instrument; someone laughing or crying; a police car or ambulance; starting up your car; someone sneezing or blowing a nose; the voices of everyone in your family (with matching photos). In fact the possibilities are endless, but start with just a few. You will find that even when your child knows exactly what the familiar sounds are, he will enjoy playing the game over and over again.

Picture cube

Select a large cube-shaped cardboard box next time you visit the supermarket. Seal up all the flaps and stick one large picture, cut out of a magazine, on to each of the six sides. 'Throw' the picture cube like a dice to see which item is facing upwards. Your child will enjoy calling out the name of the picture as well as rolling the 'dice'. You could even have a matching picture or a matching object to run and get when the appropriate picture 'comes up'.

Telephones

Children of this age love playing with toy telephones and will chatter into them, reflecting the up and down nature of talking. You may even hear those first social words, 'hello' and 'bye-bye'. during this game. If you have two toy telephones, you can pretend to speak to each other on them. You can make your own telephone out of a small box with a lid. Draw buttons on to the box and cut the lid into a receiver shape.

Sort it

Get your child to sort items into groups – perhaps she could put all her cars in one box and all her books into another, for example. Sometimes sorting comes up naturally in everyday situations, so when you're doing the washing ask your child to find all the socks or perhaps all *her* things, talking about the different clothes as you do it.

Nursery rhymes

Your child will love the rhythm and sound of nursery rhymes, even though the individual words may mean very little to him. Children love their familiarity so don't worry about singing the same ones over and over again. Try leaving off the last word or phrase for your child to say, for example 'We all fall ____.' or 'Humpty Dumpty sat on a ____.' You could also try singing action songs such as

'Here we go round the mulberry bush' and get your child to join in the actions. As you sing it, he can also decide which action you are going to do next.

Scrap books

Let your child choose which pictures she would like in her scrap book and help her stick them in. She may want to include photographs of people in the family. She may enjoy sorting pictures into categories first, putting all the people on one page and all the pictures of toys on another page, for example. This is a useful exercise in logical thinking which will help her with language development.

Books

This is the age when children become increasingly interested in books, so join the library and choose plastic and board books if they are likely to get torn. You needn't restrict yourself to books – your child will enjoy looking at catalogues, magazines or large, clear pictures stuck on to card and covered with clear plastic. At this stage, choose books with clear pictures of everyday objects. Your child will not be able to follow a story as such and complicated pictures with a lot of small details will be too much for him. Your child will learn many of his new words from books. After all, many children learn the word for, say, 'elephant' long before they've seen a real one.

Questions ... questions ... questions ...

❛ My fourteen-month-old is not saying words at all even though his friends of the same age are. Is he backward in any way? ❜

FIRST WORDS

The age when children learn their first words is very variable and will be affected by many factors; girls generally talk earlier than boys, first-born children earlier than their brothers and sisters, or perhaps there has been a history of ear problems which affected hearing earlier on. However, some children just start later than others for no obvious reason. It is by no means an indication of low intelligence or anything being wrong. At fourteen months, the chances are that your child will catch up with his friends once he gets going. Of course it has been shown that the amount a child is talked to has an effect on language development, so do set aside part of the day for talking together and looking at books. But you can only provide the input – you cannot *make* your child say words, they will come just as soon as he is ready.

If your child has frequent coughs and colds and particularly if he has a tendency towards ear infections, it may be worth discussing this with your GP or health visitor. In the meantime, try not to compare your child with others but concentrate on what he can do and enjoy watching him develop.

If your child still has no words once he has passed eighteen months and certainly if he is still not speaking as he approaches his second birthday, then ask your health visitor to refer you to a speech and language therapist who will monitor progress (see Chapter 11).

> *My eighteen-month-old has plenty of words and I can easily understand her. But nobody else can! Should I start to correct her?*

No, it is quite normal for a child's first words to be unclear but at this stage it doesn't really matter. She does have her own pattern of speaking which is why you can usually understand her. For example, she probably always says 't' instead of a hard 'c' so that 'cup' is always 'tup' and 'cat' is always 'tat'. You will also find that she tends to talk about what is happening at that moment or about the things around her so you should be able to make some good guesses. As she says more and as she matures, so the sounds of speech will continue to develop and her words will gradually become clearer. In the meantime, don't correct her as she would soon get the message that she is doing something wrong which will put her off speaking altogether. Instead, make sure she hears the correct versions straight away. For example, if she says 'tat', reply 'Yes, there's a *cat*. The cat's sitting on the chair.'

> ❝ My child seems to have forgotten some of the words she knew. She used to say 'dolly' all the time but she hasn't said it for weeks now. ❞

Children at this one-word stage often seem to go through a period when it seems that when one word is learnt, another is lost. In fact, the words have not been lost or forgotten – your child still understands the 'lost' words and will soon begin to use them again in exactly the same way. It is not known exactly why this happens but it is as though a child has to concentrate hard on the new ones, practising and reinforcing them all the time. Once your child starts to put words together, this probably won't happen any more. In the meantime, don't try to make your child say the words you know she knows, let her spend some time on the new ones.

> ❝ How can I get my child to learn new words? Should I avoid introducing long words which may be difficult for him to say? ❞

Your child won't necessarily be put off by long words or words with complicated sequences of sounds. Few children in their second year will be able to pronounce 'squirrel' as an adult would but will nevertheless attempt the word if they want to say it. Children of this age are unaware of the 'mistakes' they make and naturally assume we must know what they are talking about.

Once your child has started to use words, there is little you can do to stop him learning new ones. Keep talking about what you're doing, keep on looking at books, and involve your child in your day-to-day activities. Make use of trips out to the park or the beach or wherever to talk about things he won't see at home – the sea, sand, roundabouts etc. Even a walk along the road means you'll be talking about all sorts of different things – the flowers, trees, lamp posts, letter boxes and so on.

❝ *How long should I talk to my child for?* **❞**

There are no set rules on this but you will probably find that talking tends to come in short bursts which will suit your child's attention span at this time. For example, you may have a chat in the morning when your child wakes up, then she may play on her own while you get dressed. This may be followed by a short discussion over breakfast, then another break while you wash up. Then one parent may talk and play with her while the other gets an older child ready for school and so on. Talking happens most of the time in a busy household but do remember to let your child have some time on her own, not only so she can become involved in other activities, but so that she can talk to herself. These 'practice sessions' seem to be very important to children of this age.

Try not to talk until your face goes blue and your child has become bored and restless. Always stop on a happy note when you are both enjoying yourselves. That way you will both look forward to your next chat.

❝ *Does it matter if I use baby talk? I just seem to say 'doggie' and 'gee-gee' automatically.* **❞**

It doesn't matter too much – many children seem to have thrived on endless baby talk – but it does mean your child has to switch to the adult form later on. 'Gee-gee' may sound quite cute from a one-year-old but it sounds extremely babyish from a four- or five-year-old.

The main argument against baby talk is that you might just as well use the 'proper' words in the first place and that way your child will, hopefully, be hearing the same words from everyone. Another negative aspect of baby talk is to actually over-simplify the structure of our sentences so that they are not really being said correctly. For example, you may find yourself saying 'Baby want milk?' instead of 'Do you want some milk?' This may not matter too much in the early stages but it is a habit which some parents find difficult to change once their child starts using sentences. Also, remember that your child is learning about sentences long before he is able to use them himself.

You may find yourself talking to your child in an exaggerated sing-song manner but there is nothing wrong with this. In fact it will help to hold your child's attention and will serve to emphasise those key words of the sentence. But do try and cut down on the 'doggies' and 'gee-gees' and get your partner and friends to remind you.

CHAPTER FOUR

Putting words together (two to three years)

At age two, some children will already be stringing words together in short sentences while others may still be using one word at a time. But during the year your child is likely to have a great spurt in talking so that by the age of three she will be using sentences of three or four words and you'll find yourself having quite sophisticated conversations with her.

First 'sentences' will be made up of two words and your child will spend many weeks at this two-word stage before adding an extra word, gradually progressing to longer and more complicated sentences. He won't bother with the little, unimportant words of speech – a, the, in, but, they etc. – but will string together the two key words in the message he is trying to convey. For example, you won't hear your two-year-old saying 'Daddy is at the shops', he will leave out those three insignificant words in the middle and say 'Daddy shops'. And you'll know exactly what he means.

At this stage, your child will also miss out those little word endings so that she won't say 'Baby cried' or 'Jane's hopping' but is more likely to say 'Baby cry' or 'Jane hop'. However, she will start to use word endings soon after reaching the two-word stage, firstly adding the 's' on the end where there is more than one thing – cats, dogs etc. Then she will use 'ing' – running, jumping and so on. Even if you ask your child to repeat a sentence after you such

TALKING AND YOUR CHILD

as 'Daddy's gone to work', she will reduce it to her own level and say 'Daddy work' back to you. Many two-year-olds will often echo the last word or two of what you say so that when you tell her to 'Take your socks off', you will hear a little voice saying 'Socks off' back to you. However, her sentences won't just be repetitions of what you say, she will be creating sentences all of her own. After all, she's hardly likely to have copied 'Allgone milk' or 'More teatime' directly from you.

In English, the order of the words in sentences is very important. 'John likes Jane' means something different from 'Jane likes John' and 'Man bites dog' is certainly not the same as 'Dog bites man'. Even in this early stage, your child will always get his words in the right order. So if he wants to tell you that Daddy is having a wash, he will say 'Daddy wash' but if he wants to tell you that he's going to wash Daddy's face for him, he will say 'Wash Daddy'. This is worth remembering when you are trying to work out what your child is trying to tell you. So if, for example, he says 'Go car', then he is likely to be asking you if he can go in the car and not commenting on the fact that the car is going somewhere – that would be 'Car go'.

Questions also start to appear at this stage, usually beginning with 'where' or 'what' and occasionally 'who'. 'Where teddy?' 'Where Daddy?' and, of course 'What's that?' are typical. At the same time, your child will be asking some questions just by using a rising tone in her voice. 'Mummy work?' can easily be identified as a question if your child ends the sentence on a higher note and has the accompanying questioning look on her face. She will not yet change the order of words to form a sentence as in 'Can I . . . ?' or 'Is Mummy . . . ?'

At age two, your child will start to refer to himself by name and will also begin to say 'Me' and 'You' and sometimes 'I'. By the age of three, your child will have a vocabulary of several hundred words and will put three or four words together into a simple sentence. These longer sentences will still only contain key words and simplified grammar such as 'Me go shops.'

Early sentences

When your child seems to be stuck using one word at a time, there are several clues which will tell you that sentences are just around the corner.

- Your child will use a sequence of single words – not linked together as a sentence because of the break between each one, but nevertheless referring to the same thing. For example, your child might say 'Baby. Juice. Wet.' – still single words but telling you that her baby sister has spilled her juice down herself and got wet.
- You may hear your child say a piece of jargon or a nonsense word followed by a real word, for example, 'Arer Teddy'.
- Some children start to say words like 'cats' with the 's' on the end to indicate more than one. This also means sentences are not far away.
- Your child may have a sudden increase in the number of words he says and start to use different types of words – not just naming words but action words (give, pull) and descriptive words.

Daddy car . . .

Two-word sentences can tell us an awful lot. If you listen to which word is stressed, or sounds louder, you can tell a lot about what your child means. For example, '*Daddy* car' might mean 'I want Daddy to drive the car' or even 'I want to go in Daddy's car' whereas 'Daddy *car*' might mean 'Daddy, will you pass me my toy car.'

'Daddy car' could also mean any one of the following: 'Daddy is in the car', 'Daddy has just arrived home in the car', 'This is Daddy's car', 'This is a big car' (a daddy car), 'Daddy, will you get in the car?', 'Is this Daddy's car?' You will still need to rely on the situation together with your child's gestures to decipher exactly what she is telling you.

Telegram speech

If you were sending a telegram or putting an advert in the paper where you had to pay for each word, you would find there were a lot of words you could miss out of an ordinary sentence without really changing the meaning. A telegram announcing that your father had arrived would not need to say 'My father has now arrived' when two words could say the same thing. In the same way, your child reduces the message to 'Daddy here'. The words that you would miss out for an advert or telegram are the same words that your child misses out at this stage. So listen out for phrases like 'Mummy socks', 'Give Teddy drink' and 'Me want milk'.

Your child's sentences

Listen carefully and you'll notice that your child's phrases are made up of different sorts of words to give you a variety of information. The following types of two-word sentences are the most common:

- Telling you about something or someone carrying out an action, e.g. 'Jenny run'.
- Telling you about two people, or things, which are relating to each other in some way, e.g. 'Mummy car'.
- Telling you about an action carried out on a person or thing, e.g. 'Give shoe'.
- Telling you that something's there, e.g. 'That book'.
- Telling you that something's not there, e.g. 'Allgone milk'.
- Requesting more of something, e.g. 'Book again' or 'More milk'.
- Telling you about an action relating to a place, e.g. 'Go road'.
- Telling you about where something is, e.g. 'Jumper chair'.
- Telling you that something belongs to someone, e.g. 'Mummy hat'.
- Giving you a description of something, e.g. 'Big boat'.

What two- to three-year-olds can understand

Your two-year-old will understand several hundred words and will be able to follow simple instructions. For the first months following her second birthday, you will need to restrict what you talk about to the 'here and now', with limited references to what has already happened. But once she is three, she will be able to understand longer and more complicated sentences and you can talk to her about past events and make future plans. At the beginning of this year, your child will still be at the picture book stage but as she approaches the age of three, she will be able to follow simple familiar stories such as 'The Three Bears'.

At two, your child will be understanding instructions involving two key words such as 'Put the *cup* in the *cupboard*'. He will understand the meaning of some action words, particularly ones he can carry out himself such as 'run', 'sleep' and 'drink'. During this year, his memory and concentration will improve and he will start to have an understanding of colours, size and the position of things.

Colours

Between the ages of two and three, your child will learn to match colours – putting all the red things in one box and all the blue things in another one, for example. By age three, she will know the words for red, green, blue and yellow but she may still confuse them.

Size

Your child will understand the more general terms, 'big' and 'little', first. Specific terms such as 'tall' and 'short' or 'wide' and 'narrow' will come much later. Before he is able to say 'big' or 'little' appropriately himself, he needs to understand exactly what they mean. At this stage, he will notice that some things are bigger than others, that he can't wear Mummy's coat or that the big brick won't fit into the tiny box. He will tend to see things as big or little in relation to his own size – an elephant is big and a mouse is little. But it will take longer for him to realise that one mouse can be bigger than another. He will also begin to use words like 'more' and 'lots'.

Position

The first position words your child will understand are 'in', 'on' and 'under'. Other words such as 'behind', 'next to' and 'in front' won't mean much to her yet.

Groups

Your two-year-old will begin to see that items, and pictures, can be sorted into categories – food, animals, clothes and so on.

What to say to your two-year-old

Praise what your child has said and add the missing bits in your next sentence. For example, if your child says 'Dog eat dinner', you might say 'Yes, the dog's eating his dinner.' Then add some more information such as 'It's meat today.' Ask your child different types of questions while you are playing or looking at books. 'What's that?' is both simple and boring for two- to three-year-olds, so vary your questions by asking 'What's he doing?', 'What do you do with that?' and 'Where does that go?' 'Why' questions are too difficult at this stage.

Don't anticipate your child's every need. If you give her a drink at regular intervals, she will never have the need to ask for one. Also, make sure you have your child's full attention before you talk to her. Children of this age may become so engrossed in a toy that they are unable to listen to anyone speaking. If your child fits this description, call her name first and get her to look at you before you speak. If your child seems to switch off while you are talking to her, perhaps you are using sentences which are too long or complicated. You will still need to keep what you say to a fairly simple level.

Remember that your child is learning new words and ideas all the time from you. There is no need to sit down and teach your child the words 'big' and 'little' for example. These words will occur quite naturally when you are laying the table or hanging out the washing. Just emphasise and repeat any words or ideas which you think may be new or difficult for your child.

The sounds of speech

Your child's words will gradually become clearer as she develops, although immaturities are still quite normal. Of course, there are individual variations and your child will develop at her own rate. Even so, the majority of children learn the sounds of speech in roughly the same order. The following are usually mastered by age two: *p, t, b, d, n, m, w* and vowel sounds (*a, e, ee, ah*, etc.).

A two-year-old may have difficulty with *s, f, k* (or hard *c*), *g, l, y, r, sh, ch, j, th* as well as blends of sounds such as *st, pl, gl, cr*. Some ends of words may be left off, so typically, words may be pronounced as follows: 'sun' as 'dun'; 'cup' as 'tup'; 'fish' as 'fis' or 'pis'; 'go' as 'doe'; 'run' as 'wun'; 'chair' as 'tair'; 'stop' as 'top', and 'plate' as 'pate'.

Sounds will also be missed out of longer words or sometimes the sounds will be made in the wrong order, so 'aeroplane' may be pronounced 'epane' and 'hospital' may be pronounced as 'hopsital' or 'hopital'.

By the age of three, your child will probably be using *s* and *f* and sometimes *g* and *k*. But blends of sounds will still be reduced so that 'glue' will be 'goo' and 'smoke' will be 'moke'. Syllables may be left out of longer words so that 'elephant' becomes 'efent' and 'helicopter' may be 'copter'. *Sh, ch, th, j* and *r* will not be present for some time yet, and *l* and *y* may also be missing.

You should be able to understand your child's speech most of the time although there will still be occasions when your child attempts a long or particularly difficult word and the result will keep you guessing. Luckily, in these instances, your child will rarely feel it is her bad pronunciation but will blame you for your stupidity in not understanding her!

> ### At a glance: what your two-and-a-half-year-old can do
>
> - Say more than 200 words.
> - Put words together and tell you about, or ask for, anything she wants. If she doesn't know the word she will get round it by using words she does know. If she doesn't know the word for 'breakfast', she'll say 'dinner', if she can't say 'more please', then she'll say 'again'.
> - Know his own name.
> - Follow your simple instructions such as 'Hang your coat up', 'Put your jumper on the bed' or 'Bring me your empty cup'. This is obviously useful to both of you.
> - Sing a good selection of nursery rhymes.
> - Play meaningfully with small toys such as doll's house furniture.
> - Ask questions beginning with 'what', 'where' and 'who'.
> - Enjoy books with more detailed pictures; may even follow a simple story.
> - Still talk to himself at play and still echo back what you have said.
> - Love having a chat with you.

Mind your Ps and Qs

Can you really expect your two-year-old who has just started to talk to say 'please' and 'thank you'? When is the right time to introduce these useful and essential little words, and is 'ta' as good as the real thing? Here are some thoughts on the whole question of courtesy words.

You can say please and thank you long before your child is saying words at all. Your child will always understand more than she says and it's never too early to set an example. When your child is at the repetitive stage, at around eighteen months, she will happily repeat 'please' and 'thank you' after you, so encourage her to do so and a good habit may become established.

Don't worry *how* he says 'please' and 'thank you' so long as *you* say them correctly, any approximation from your child is acceptable at this stage. Don't *make* your child say please and thank you at this stage. It will only serve to create temper tantrums and put her off altogether. If she does say 'please' before you hand her a drink, then praise her. If not, say it for her and then try again next time. 'Thank you' is difficult for a young child to say so 'ta' is perfectly acceptable. If you continue to say thank you, she will start to use the correct form when she is ready.

There's no reason why 'please' and 'thank you' shouldn't be amongst your child's first words. He won't yet have any sense of being polite but will say them to please you or even to get what he wants. Hopefully by the age of three or four, your child will say these words as an automatic response. The courtesy aspect comes later.

Games and activities

Make-a-sentence picture book

This is a game to encourage your child to put words together. Make a book by sticking large pieces of paper together, then cut across horizontally, half-way down the book so that it is almost in two halves. Stick photos of people or pictures of animals on the top half-pages and pictures of food, toys or vehicles on the bottom half-pages. You can then create different sentences by turning over either the top or the bottom half-page of the book. For example, you could have a picture of Daddy at the top and cake at the bottom for 'Daddy eats cake'. Turn over the top half for, say 'Mummy eats cake' and the bottom half for 'Mummy eats sausages'. Obviously, children at the two-word stage are more likely to say 'Daddy cake' and 'Mummy sausages'.

Moving pictures

By cutting out an arm or a leg and attaching it to a picture of a person using a brass paper fastener, the pictures can be made to perform actions. A picture of a girl can be made to kick a ball, bang a drum or wave goodbye which will encourage the use of these phrases.

Hide-it

Your child will now be learning all about position words – 'in', 'on', 'under', 'next to' etc. Encourage your child by getting her to hide her toys or herself in, on or under large cardboard boxes. You could try drawing a picture of someone hiding under a box or a table which your child can then attempt to copy by hiding under a real box or table.

Tea sets

These are ideal for learning about size, colour and shape. Different sized plates, spoons and cups can be sorted so that big teddies have the big items and little teddies have the smaller ones. Encourage your child to talk about teddy's plate, dolly's cup and so on. You could also make different sorts (and sizes) of food together out of playdough.

Miming

Cut out pictures from magazines of people carrying out various activities such as running, cooking or kicking a ball. Mime the action on the picture to see if your child can guess what you are doing. Let her have a go at miming as well.

Function picture lotto

Give your child a lotto board with six or eight pictures on it. You have the matching individual pictures, then ask your child to find the right picture by describing what you do with it. For example, you might say 'Which one do we eat?', 'Which one do we cut with?' or 'Which one do we play with?' When your child points to the right picture, she then 'wins' the matching one to put on her board.

Action songs

Tune up your voice as these are good for teaching new words, for encouraging your child to listen and just for having a good time. A good one is 'Heads, shoulders, knees and toes' as this is the age for learning body parts. Also try 'Teddy bear, teddy bear'. If you don't know the tune, just say the rhyme and do the actions:

Teddy bear, teddy bear touch your nose;
Teddy bear, teddy bear touch your toes.
Teddy bear, teddy bear turn around;
Teddy bear, teddy bear touch the ground.
Teddy bear, teddy bear go upstairs;
Teddy bear, teddy bear say your prayers.
Teddy bear, teddy bear turn out the light;
Teddy bear, teddy bear say good night.

Another good action song is 'Miss Polly':

Miss Polly had a dolly who was sick, sick sick (pretend to rock baby in your arms);
So she called for the doctor to come quick, quick, quick (mime dialling).
The doctor came with his bag (lift hand as if holding bag) *and his hat* (point to head);

And he knocked on the door with a rat-a-tat-tat (mime
knocking on door).
He looked at the dolly and he shook his head (shake head);
And he said 'Miss Polly, put her straight to bed' (shake
finger).
He wrote on a paper for a pill, pill, pill (mime writing);
'I'll be back in the morning if she's still ill'.

'The wheels on the bus', 'Ten in the bed' and 'Incy wincy spider'
are other favourites. Many libraries stock books and tapes of action
songs which you could borrow. Some children are able to string
more words together when they are singing than during conversations.

Silly pairs

Using magazine or catalogue pictures stuck on to card, make two
sets of cards, one with people or animals and one with objects.
Lay the two sets of cards face down and turn over one card from
each set encouraging your child to make a sentence out of them.
For example, you might turn over a picture of a teddy and then a
picture of a plate of food for 'Teddy eating'. Some 'sentences' might
be quite silly such as 'A dog cooking' or 'A fish climbing a ladder'
which should add to the enjoyment of the game.

Books

Books are not just for reading to your child. Let her join in with the
story or comment on the pictures. Looking at books together usually
means talking together so make it part of your routine, perhaps at
the end of the day.

A two-year-old will enjoy simple picture books, but gradually
introduce books with pictures of people doing things rather than
just pictures of individual items. Many children of this age particularly enjoy books featuring photographs of other children doing
familiar activities such as going to the park or getting dressed. And

don't forget to look through your own photograph albums together.

At around two-and-a-half to three, you can introduce your child to simple repetitive stories such as 'The Three Bears', 'The Three Little Pigs' or 'The Gingerbread Man'. Encourage him to join in with the repetitive lines, for example, 'I'll huff and I'll puff and I'll . . .', 'Run, run as fast as you can, you can't catch me I'm the . . .' and 'Who's been sitting on . . .'

Put it there

It's important to encourage your child to listen to what you have to say as well as encouraging her to talk herself. So play a game where you give her instructions but don't make them too obvious. She may not have to listen too carefully if you say 'Sit dolly on the chair' if this is where dolly always sits. But if you say 'Put dolly on the table' or 'Put dolly under the chair', then she has to listen to every part of the instruction. To make this game more interesting, you could get your child to put another brick on the tower or a piece in the puzzle every time she gets it right.

Questions ... questions ... questions ...

❛ My two-year-old child seems to have a lot of words but shows no inclination to put them together into sentences. How can I help him? ❜

Some children start off by having a wide range of names for things before they start to use different types of words. Although naming words are often put together into short sentences – 'Daddy chair', 'Teddy bed' – it helps if you introduce different sorts of words to your child at the one-word stage. A good vocabulary of action words and description words gives your child more opportunity to use phrases of two words. So as you go about your daily routine, start to put the emphasis on what you are doing or what things look like rather than just their names. For example each morning, you might make a point of emphasising and repeating the familiar phrases – 'Washing your face', 'Cleaning your teeth' and 'Combing your hair'. You could even lead your child in by saying 'Mummy's combing her hair, Daddy's combing his hair and John is . . .' You cannot make your child put words together but you can make sure he is hearing plenty of short phrases made up of familiar words. Look at books and play with miniature people to give you plenty of opportunity to say these phrases and very soon your child will be saying them too.

My two-year-old is difficult to understand, mainly because she leaves all the ends off her words. Will she grow out of this?

Yes, she probably will but there are steps you can take to help her on her way. It is very common for two-year-olds to leave some sounds out, particularly if she has only recently started using words but this should gradually improve during this year. When your child says a word, omitting the end, make sure you repeat the word back to her so she is always hearing the correct form. For example, if she says 'My boo', you might say 'Yes, that's your *boot* – shall we put it on?' You could also play a listening game to encourage her to listen to the ends of words. For example, you could look at a picture book and get your child to tell you if you are saying the word correctly or not. 'Boot' would be right and 'Boo' would be wrong. Once your child can hear the difference, she will find your mistakes very amusing. Another game would involve thinking of pairs of words which are the same except for the last sound, for example car and cart. Draw a picture for each word and see if your child can put a counter on the one you say. Other pairs you could use include: sew and soap; bow and boat; go and goat; sea and seat; lie and light; lay and lane; me and meat; pea and piece; no and nose; pie and pile; ray and rake; tea and team; toe and toast.

Try to pick words that your child already knows the meaning of.

PUTTING WORDS TOGETHER

There is no need to get your child to try to say words properly or to correct her at this stage. Just give her plenty of listening practice.

> ❝ My two-year-old has quite a few words and even puts them together sometimes. However, she is not always easy to understand and as a result gets very frustrated. This leads to temper tantrums with my child refusing to repeat her request. ❞

A child just beginning to put phrases together can communicate a lot of information and requests but she does rely on a certain amount of interpretation from you. Take note of where she's pointing or looking as she is likely to be talking about something that's right there in front of you. Then take a calculated guess. Stop what you are doing and give her your full attention so that she knows she has plenty of time to get her message across. A certain amount of frustration is inevitable but it does get easier as you get used to your child's own individual way of talking and as her language develops.

Make sure you spend a short time each day looking at books together. You will know what she's talking about because she can point it out in the book and this will give her confidence with her talking.

> ❝ My child never seems to listen to me. When he's playing with his favourite toys, he doesn't even move when I call him for dinner or a drink. I know he can hear so what's wrong? ❞

It is quite normal for a two- or three-year-old to go through a long stage of rigid concentration. During his first year, you probably noticed that he was easily distracted by the slightest noise, by someone coming into the room or even by a different toy suddenly coming into view. Now he seems to cut everything else out and concentrate just on the matter in hand. It is important to get your child's attention before you speak to him and this means making sure he is looking at your face. Even when you are playing with him, he may find it difficult to listen to you or follow your instructions while he is engaged in play. So again, make sure you have his full attention first. Usually from about three years, he will begin to find listening easier.

Some two-year-olds still have very fleeting attention and will flit from toy to toy, hardly concentrating for more than a minute. In this case, you need to build up your child's attention span gradually. Encourage him to finish each task but don't expect too much to start with – just a simple puzzle perhaps. Once he can finish a two-minute task, introduce an activity which takes slightly longer. But remember, don't expect too much, two-year-olds play very hard and may need to run around for part of the day, not having to concentrate on anything.

> *My child has a lot of coughs, colds and earaches. Should I worry if his ears become blocked and will it affect his speech now he has started talking?*

You should always take your child to your GP with ear problems and ask for a hearing check if you are at all worried. Some children with frequent blocked ears and ear infections suffer from fluctuating hearing loss. They can hear normally when they are well but their hearing becomes dulled during these bouts of illness. If the illnesses are frequent this needs to be discussed with the doctor as it can indeed affect speech development. Your child may have difficulty hearing particular sounds just at the age when he is learning to produce these sounds himself. If his speech does fall behind or become unclear then he still has every chance of 'catching up' once his hearing problems have been rectified. But the sooner the better. In the meantime, you can try to compensate a little when you feel his ears are blocked or infected. No need to shout but choose times when you can sit close by him and talk clearly. If one ear tends to be affected more than the other, then sit on his 'good' side and carry on talking and chatting to your child as much as possible.

PUTTING WORDS TOGETHER

Some of my child's words for things are so cute that we have all started using them. Now an orange is an 'ongaz', a television is a 'tever' and my son Christopher is always known as 'Kipper'. Is there any harm in this?

It is lovely to be able to enjoy your child's way of talking but what might sound cute from a two-year-old, will sound immature or even irritating by the time he is five. By adopting his words, you are not really giving him the opportunity to hear the correct form which he will then use himself once he is ready. Sorry, using his version is not going to help your child, so when he says 'ongaz', you say 'orange'. However, you will want to remember this delightful stage so make a tape recording of your child and you can both look back and laugh in years to come.

CHAPTER FIVE

Learning the rules
(three to four years)

You will now feel that your child is no longer a baby or a toddler but a little person, especially now she has begun to talk in sentences. She will be putting three or four words together, will be able to say at least 1000 words and will understand even more. She will still be leaving out a lot of little unimportant words and using simplified grammar, leaving off many word endings, but this will change a great deal during this year. Typically, a three-year-old may well say 'Me play John', whereas a four-year-old is more likely to say 'I played with John.' The message is the same, but by age four she is including the '-ed' ending to indicate that she has already played with John and the word 'with' to make the sentence more complete. Learning all about grammar is a natural process for your child at this stage. You won't have to sit down and teach your child all the rules, as she will be learning all the time from her many conversations with you and other important people in her life including other children of her own age. She will have progressed from just grabbing a toy from another child and saying 'No' or 'Mine' and will now start to play and talk with other children in a much more social manner. There is no doubt that nursery or playgroup will now provide an important setting for your child to develop her communication skills as well as giving her the opportunity to socialise and make friends. Play, socialising and language development are all closely linked and will develop alongside each other during these pre-school years.

Your child will now begin to talk about past events and make future plans so your conversations together will no longer be restricted to the here and now – what you are doing at that moment or the books and toys in front of you. You will be able to talk more easily about your trip to the zoo yesterday, what you had for breakfast this morning or what you might do next weekend. And you will feel that you are talking to your child on equal terms. It won't just be you starting off the conversation or asking questions; your child will also be asking his share of questions – in fact probably more than his share! And he will be able to start the conversation off or change the subject himself. By age four your child may still be making 'errors', both with grammar and with speech sounds, but these certainly won't stop him communicating in quite a sophisticated and mature way.

Rules and regulations

When children first start to talk about the past or use plurals (to indicate more than one thing) or indeed to use any of those grammatical endings which are so complicated in the English language, they get it right. Between the ages of about three and three-and-a-half, you may well hear your child say sentences like 'I went to Grandma's', 'Look at my feet' or 'I ran home'. She will have imitated, quite successfully, your versions of the past tense (went, ran), plurals (feet) and so on. Suddenly, she will progress to learning the rules of grammar but will apply those rules to *irregular* verbs, resulting in words like 'goed'.

You may be left wondering if your child has gone backwards. For now she will be saying 'I goed to Grandma's', 'Look at my foots' and 'I runned home' because we *usually* put 'ed' on the end of a word to denote past time (jump<u>ed</u>, hopp<u>ed</u>) and an 's' on the end to indicate more than one (boot<u>s</u>, cow<u>s</u>). However, this is a

60

TALKING AND YOUR CHILD

sign of progress, because your child has obviously become aware of how words should be made up and is not just copying you. She will carry on making these grammatical errors until she's about five, gradually using the right forms without anyone having to teach her.

You can prove that your child has suddenly latched on to the rules of English with a simple experiment. Draw a funny animal or monster and call it by a nonsense word, say, a 'bup' or a 'dill'. Then draw lots of them in a group and say 'Here is one bup and here are lots of ____'. Your child is sure to fill in the word 'bups' even though there is no such word. She knows that you put an 's' on the end of a word when there is more than one. The exceptions such as 'sheep' will be 'sheeps' during this stage of learning the rules. Similarly, you can tell a story about a man who likes to 'flep'. When you say 'Today, he is flepping, yesterday he ____', your child will say 'flepped'.

Awareness of these rules of grammar gradually develops between the ages of two and five, or even later. By the age of three, your child will probably already use the '-ing' ending as in 'running' and the plural 's' as in 'cats'. She may even use the possessive 's' as in 'Mummy's car'. Gradually, more will be added and most children acquire these little parts of language in much the same order. Roger Brown, in 1973, found the order in which children learn the rules to be as follows:

1 '-ing' e.g. 'Mummy running'
2 'In', 'on' e.g. 'on box', in house'
3 Plural 's' as in 'my cats'
4 Irregular past tense e.g. 'sang', 'went', 'made'
5 Possessive 's' (meaning belonging to) e.g. 'Mummy's coat'
6 'Is' e.g. 'Mummy is pretty'
7 'A' and 'The' e.g. 'Give me the book'
8 Regular past tense (the 'ed' ending) e.g. 'I skipped'
9 's' on the end of a verb e.g. 'He kicks', 'She likes'
10 '-es' on the end of a verb e.g. 'He catches', 'She watches'
11 'Has' e.g. 'She has walked'

12 's' as a shortened version of 'is' e.g. 'Daddy's here'
13 's' as a shortened version of 'has' e.g. 'She's walked'
14 Superlatives e.g. 'biggest', 'best'
15 Comparatives e.g. 'taller', 'bigger'
16 Words ending in '-ly' to describe how something is done e.g. 'slowly', 'quietly'.

Many children are not able to use the last six or seven of these until they are nearer the age of five. Certainly your child will go on making mistakes until he is five or even six although the 'errors' will gradually become restricted to more complicated sentences or unusual words.

The things they say . . .

All the following sentences have been heard by children at this level and demonstrate some of the typical 'mistakes' made by three-year-olds.

'I want more macaronis in my bowl.'
'Not give me that.'
'There some pencil. Give me pencil. I want write now.'
'I wented to Jack's party. Got a party bag.'
'I go shops, no.'
'When you get my drink, Mummy?'
'Nother one biscuit on my plate (for) me.'
'I getted a new farm now. I got cows and sheeps and hens and tractors.'
'Pink rabbit go sleep my bed.'
'You pick it ups and put it there.'
'I got a headache in my foot.'

'But why, Mummy?'

At age two, your child may have started to ask the typical question 'What's that?' and this seemingly continuous question will carry on all year. Other sorts of questions will also appear, particularly those beginning with 'Where?' and 'Who?' At first your child won't be able to change the order of words, so he will ask questions such as 'Where you are going?' and 'Who that is?' However, by age four, this begins to change and he is more likely to say 'Where are you going?' and 'Who is that?' 'Why' questions tend to come much later, and although you may hear your child ask 'Why', she won't really know what answer to expect, as she still hasn't fully grasped what 'why' means. This will become clear when you ask *her* a 'why' question as you probably won't get the answer you want. But remember, children learn by listening to you and experimenting with the language they have. So if your child says 'Why?', do answer her appropriately, even though your answer is likely to be followed by another 'Why?'

As your child starts to talk about past events and future plans, he may start to ask questions beginning with 'When?' But his understanding of time may not yet be very precise and 'last week' may mean the same to him as 'yesterday'.

The other type of questions we ask are where the word order is changed – 'Are you coming?', 'Is that your book?' and so on. At first your child will leave the word order the same – 'You are coming?' – but you will know it's a question because of the tone of her voice and the rising pattern of speech. However, during this third year, your child will start to use the right word order when asking this type of question.

You may find that your child asks a continuous stream of questions even when he already knows the answers. When he asks 'What's that?' for the umpteenth time and you know he knows, it's difficult not to lose your patience. But you could always reply to his question with another question, politician-style. So when he says 'What's that?', you could reply 'Well what do you think it is?' There seem to be two reasons for this trend of asking unnecessary questions. Firstly, your three-year-old loves practising his new language skills, and secondly, he enjoys talking with you so much, he wants to keep the conversation going. He knows that when all else fails a quick 'Why?' will get you chatting again straight away. Don't forget, as well, that he may be copying you. You will certainly be asking him questions to which you know the answer. 'What's that?', 'What colour is it?' and so on. So why shouldn't he do the same?

'No I won't'

Your two-year-old will have had a lot of practice with negative words – 'no', 'won't' and 'not' are often used quite early on and are very useful for those typical 'terrible' twos. At three, your child will have fewer temper tantrums, but her ways of saying 'no' become more sophisticated.

To start with, she will simply latch 'no' or 'not' on to the beginning or end of a sentence. 'No juice, Mummy', 'Not go shops' or 'Have biscuit – no' are all typical utterances. Next come 'don't' and 'can't' which are just used at the beginning of the sentence to start with – 'Can't see me', 'Don't want it' etc. Gradually, the fuller versions of these sentences are used and 'can't' and 'don't' will then be put in the right place within a sentence – 'I don't like cabbage', 'I can't do it' etc.

What three- to four-year-olds understand

Your child will continue with the trend of understanding a lot more than he is able to say himself. In fact, by age four, he will be able to follow most of what you say to him, answering your questions appropriately whether they refer to the past, present or future. Children generally understand the past before the future, but your child will have a grasp of both by about four years. You may find his concentration suddenly improves, enabling him to follow longer or more complicated sentences. He will also be able to enjoy simple stories in books or on television.

Your child will begin to understand many more words, her vocabulary increasing as she widens her world and goes out to playgroup and on trips. She will understand more words related to size – big, little, fat, short etc., position words like on, under and next to, and other descriptive words including colours. However, there will be some limitations to what your child understands. For one thing, her attention span, though improved, is still limited, so that she is likely to switch off during long, continuous adult speech. This may not be the right age to give your child a detailed account of your holiday arrangements or a lengthy speech on the starving population of the third world. You will also need to ask your three-year-old questions and get some feedback from her to ensure that she has both listened to and understood what you have said. Typically, a three-year-old may sit, apparently glued, in front of a television programme, but when questioned afterwards, it may be obvious that she has barely followed the story at all.

Three- and four-year-olds also have a tendency to repeat sentences without really understanding what they are saying. This includes echoing your speech, reciting nursery rhymes and even counting. In fact, it is often difficult to decipher exactly how much your child does understand, although he will, by now, be good at responding to other clues in your communication – gestures, tone of voice or just the situation. It is clear that by age three, it is not a good idea to talk detrimentally about your child in his presence – he might just be listening and taking it all in.

Playing away

Many children have an opportunity to start leaving mum's side occasionally during this stage. This may include going to spend a day with grandparents or playing with the child next door without an accompanying parent. For many children, it will also include going to a playgroup or nursery – a big step for both parents and child.

LEARNING THE RULES

Playgroup will give your child the chance to put her communication skills to really good use. There will be no one there who instinctively knows when she needs the toilet or which drink she prefers, so she will benefit from speaking up and using her language skills to the full. Of course, playgroup leaders and nursery teachers are trained to deal with shy and quiet children, and even the most confident child may find herself at a loss for words in such a new and perhaps strange situation. If you have been attending a toddler group, perhaps in the same premises as the playgroup, and if you are able to stay and settle your child in for the first couple of sessions, your child should soon regain her confidence. And once your child feels confident with the situation and the people caring for her, she will begin to speak with confidence, too. It has been found that during the first six months or so of playgroup or nursery, children talk far more to the adults than to the other children. However, as their fourth birthday approaches, the situation changes and most of their communication will be directed at other children.

At first your child may play alongside another child rather than *with* him, even though they may both be engaged in the same activity. Two children, at this stage, may look as though they are talking to each other, but listen closely and you will notice that each child is more or less talking to himself, so that there are two monologues going rather than a true conversation or exchange of ideas. However, gradually your child will begin to play with other children in a more cooperative way, and will use his language skills to talk about what they are doing and to discuss what else they might do. Your child will soon be chatting and joking in order to build up relationships with other children and his first real friendships will be formed. In fact, when you collect your child from playgroup, he may feel he's done enough talking for the day, and just when you want to know about his activities while you've been away, he may seem to regress to grunts and a few single words. There's nothing so infuriating as asking your child what he did, only to get a mumbled 'Nothing' or a vague 'Don't know'. But remember, your child's communication skills will have been stretched to the full, he will have played hard and he will have listened with intense concentration. So give him a chance to unwind before you expect much in the way of a chat.

The sounds of speech

Your child will be starting to use longer and more mature sentences during this year and the sounds of her speech will continue to develop in parallel to this. By age four, her speech should be totally intelligible both to people she knows and to strangers, although some immaturities still persist.

Some three-year-olds may still have difficulty with g, k, and f (saying 'date' for gate', 'bat' for 'back' and 'leas' for 'leaf'), although these are generally used correctly by about the age of three-and-a-half. 'l' may also persist as a difficult sound for part of this year. Most blends will be used correctly by three-and-a-half (spade, snow and custard) although the l may be omitted in sl, pl, bl, cl and gl. Many three- and four-year-olds will reduce clusters of three sounds to one so that words like 'splash' will be pronounced 'spash'.

At age four, ch, j, r and th are often not fully developed. There is quite a lot of variation from child to child but your child may well be able to copy sounds you say even though he does not yet use them when he's chatting normally. You may also find that he can pronounce individual words on his own quite clearly, particularly when he is copying you, but when he says the same words in general conversation, immaturities or 'mistakes' appear.

How to talk to your three-year-old

Give your child time to talk At this stage, you will find yourself asking your child endless questions, so do give her plenty of time to respond. Three-year-olds often need plenty of thinking time, so don't be too quick to answer the question yourself or bombard her with even more questions. Whenever possible, give your child your

LEARNING THE RULES

full attention when she starts the conversation off. Unfortunately, children often say the most interesting things just as you are bringing the washing in hurriedly because you're already five minutes late for the dentist. Be eight minutes late and listen to what she's got to tell you – it's very difficult at this stage to pick up the threads of the conversation later on.

Listen to your child   What your child tells you is always important to him. Let him know that it's important and interesting to you too by listening carefully to what he has to say. This will give him confidence with speaking.

Give your child plenty to talk about   We all know when our children have enjoyed a trip to the park or zoo because they'll talk about it excitedly and sometimes endlessly. New experiences give children plenty to say, so you should regard trips out, walks in the wood or a shopping expedition as a chance for a chat, both while you're doing it and after you've got home. Looking at the television and reading stories are also great conversation starters, provided the experience is a shared one.

Encourage your child to listen to you   Your child's language would not have developed this far if he hadn't been listening to you! Even so, it is important to make sure you get your child's attention before you speak. You may also find that much of the day-to-day family conversation consists of shouting out 'Who wants a drink?' or 'Come and get your dinner everyone' against a background noise of the TV or the general sound of playing. So make sure you have a quiet time for a more intimate conversation with each child sometime during the day or perhaps at bedtime.

Make sure your child has understood you   You will know if your child has fully understood your instructions by whether she carries them out correctly. If she doesn't, you may need to re-word what you have said or else avoid giving your child so much to remember at once. At other times, check that your child has understood you by asking appropriate questions. For example, if you are talking about going to the chemist for a hot water bottle, you might ask her if she knows what a hot water bottle is. You could then discuss what else you get at the chemist to ensure she understands the meaning of that too.

At a glance: what your three-and-a-half-year-old can do

- Tell you her full name, sex and age. She may even be able to tell you which town or street she lives in.
- Enjoy television programmes aimed at pre-school children.
- Use a greater variety of position words – 'in', 'on', 'behind', 'next to' etc.
- Use those words which represent people i.e. 'I', 'me', 'you', 'yours', 'she', 'he', 'it', 'his', 'her' etc.
- Talk about the past, present and future.
- Talk in sentences, sometimes of four or five words and use a wide variety of words.
- Sing many nursery rhymes with few mistakes.
- Ask questions, particularly beginning with what, where and who. Listen to the answers.
- Follow and enjoy short stories.
- Count up to ten.
- Enjoy conversations, mainly with adults but also with other children.

Games and activities

Feely bags

This game introduces descriptive words of speech. Put some every-day items into a material bag, choosing objects of different texture and shape. Ask your child to find something soft, long, round, hard etc. Then swap over so you have the feely bag and she gives you the clues.

'What's wrong?' pictures

Children of this age love things that are wrong or out of place. Drawing pictures of teddies without ears, a dog wearing wellington boots or someone with a teapot on his head will get your child using a lot of good phrases. It would be difficult for your child to describe the mistakes using just one or two words, so sentences are encouraged. Colour, size and position words can be reinforced by using pictures such as a red banana, a man with one large ear, or a cup underneath a saucer. The same game can be played using objects and toys, for example, teddy's table could be set using upside-down cups, spoons and pencils and so on.

The red red sea

A good group listening game. An adult or able child chants 'You can't get across the red, red sea unless . . .' followed by 'You've got brown shoes', 'You wear glasses' etc. (Another popular listening game is 'Simon Says'.)

Spot the mistake

Tell your child a familiar story but include some mistakes for her to listen out for. For example, in 'The Three Bears', you could say that the bears had bowls of *pencils* or that Goldilocks went to sleep *under* the bed and so on.

Find it

Hide toys around the room and ask your child to find them by giving him clues. For example, you could ask him to find something we throw, or something round. To encourage your child to listen to every word in the sentence, include negative words such as 'not' and 'don't' as in 'Find something that's not a toy'.

Give us a clue

Cut out a selection of pictures from a catalogue or magazine. Then give your child a clue such as 'It's a toy, it's yellow and you can take it to bed.' If she successfully chooses the teddy, then she 'wins' that picture and it is her turn to give you a clue.

Personal story book

Stick photos of your child at different ages in a scrap book and turn it into the story of his life so far. For example, you could have pictures of when your child first came out of hospital, when he crawled or walked, when he went on a special trip and when he went off to playschool for the first time. Children of this age love talking about themselves and this will encourage your child to talk about what has already happened using the appropriate 'past' words as he does.

Story cards

Draw pictures on individual cards which then tell a story or sequence of events. For example, you could draw a picture of your child getting out of bed, one of her having breakfast, another of her cleaning her teeth and so on. Then see if your child can put the pictures in the right order and tell the 'story'. Start with just three pictures to put in order and then increase the number to four or five. Other sequences could include:

Getting dressed   Putting pants on, putting socks on, putting a vest on, putting a dress on. More items can be added later.

Planting a seed   Planting it in the ground, a flower beginning to grow, a fully grown flower, someone picking it.

Growing up   A baby, a little toddler, a young girl, a lady.

Getting dinner ready   Buying the food, cooking it, laying the table, serving it up, eating it.

Having a bath   Getting undressed, running the bath water, washing in the bath, drying with a towel, putting pyjamas on.

Sending a letter Writing it, putting a stamp on, posting it.

These will certainly test your artistic skills but do let your child help make the cards, perhaps by colouring in some of the items.

Questions ... questions ... questions ...

> *My three-year-old seems to stammer. He repeats words over and over again and just can't get the words out. Should I tell him to slow down?*

Many children, perhaps as many as forty per cent, go through a stage where their speech is non-fluent or hesitant. Rather like stammering, words and sounds are repeated, sometimes many times and the child seems to have difficulty with 'getting his words out'. This stage can occur any time between the ages of two and six or seven, although it is most common at a time when there is a sudden increase in the amount the child is saying (often between the ages of three and four). Most children with hesitant speech pass through this stage easily and without cause for concern in a matter of months. Most will be largely unaware of their hesitant speech unless their attention is drawn to it, when they may become concerned.

Therefore ignore it where possible and never tell your child off or tell him to speak in a different way. While your child is going through this stage, ensure that you give him your full attention when he speaks, listening and commenting on what he is saying rather than how he is saying it. If your child becomes very upset or distressed about hesitant speech, contact a speech and language therapist for further advice.

> *My four-year-old knows the names of all the colours but hasn't got a clue which is which. One day he'll say his shoes are blue, the next day yellow when, in fact, they're red. Is he colour blind?*

TALKING AND YOUR CHILD

Probably not. To find out, you need to know whether he can match colours which are the same. If he can, say, put all the red toys in one box and all the blue ones in the other, then he can see the difference between those colours and is therefore not colour blind. A child may have a 'blindness' for one or two colours, perhaps red and green. Again, if he can match green items with other green items and red with red, then there is no colour blindness. Learning the names for all the colours is a more difficult task.

To start with, concentrate on matching games to help your child to look at colours. This may come up naturally in everyday situations, such as sorting out the socks or putting the crayons away. Then, while you are doing these matching activities, start to emphasise the names of two colours, perhaps red and blue. Later introduce green and yellow and concentrate on these four before introducing any others. Get your child to find something blue or red rather than constantly asking him 'What colour is it?'

> My four-year-old speaks very well except for one persisting immaturity. She still says 'Me do it' and 'Me want a biscuit' instead of using 'I'. I'm finding this impossible to correct.

This is indeed, difficult to correct. When your child says 'Me want it' and you respond with 'No, *I* want it', her reply may well be 'No, not you, *me* want it.' Immaturities in grammar don't have to be corrected in such a direct way, but your child must always hear the correct version from you. Make sure there are plenty of situations in which she is hearing you use sentences beginning with 'I' – 'I'm going to the shops', 'I've got your drink', 'I want a cup of tea' etc. *Never* revert to baby talk and say 'Mummy wants a cup of tea' or 'Mummy's got your drink.'

> My three-and-a-half-year-old has a lisp. Will she grow out of it?

Probably. A lisp is an immaturity of speech which most children grow out of quite naturally. A few do not and if it persists after the age of five or six, speech therapy advice can help. If your child enjoys looking in the mirror and making faces and noises, you could try showing her how to make a normal *s*, but don't make too much of it. She should be able to see if her tongue is poking out or not, so tell her to put her teeth together and make a snake noise. You could also try putting peanut butter or her favourite spread behind her top teeth for her to lick off. This will give her the feeling of where her tongue *should* go. If she can manage a good *s*, you can go on and try making the new 'noise' at the beginning or end of words. However, do tread carefully, make it a game and stop if it makes your child at all anxious. At this stage, you don't want to put her off talking altogether or make her feel that she's being criticised for her speech.

Some children make a rather 'slushy' *s* sound down the sides of their mouths. This is known as a lateral *s*. Again, use the peanut butter method to increase your child's awareness of her mouth. Then ask your child to make a snake noise down a straw.

‘ *My child is very chatty at home but apparently he hardly says a word at playgroup.* ’

Make sure the playgroup leader knows that your child is normally talkative at home and she will gradually help to draw your child out of his shell. Give your child plenty of time to settle in before you expect too much in the way of talking. Perhaps you could arrange to go in and help on some occasions – he may feel more confident with you in the background. You could also encourage your child to take something interesting in to show the rest of the group, as this may give him the opportunity to talk without any competition from the more confident children in the group who may not be letting him get a word in. And you could try inviting one or two of the other children home to play so that your child starts to make friends in a familiar place.

CHAPTER SIX

Stories and questions (four to five years)

By the age of four, your child probably won't need much encouragement to talk – in fact, you may not be able to stop her. She will still be making some grammatical errors such as 'I buyed some sweets' or 'I am gooder at drawing than Jane', but these will be less frequent as she gradually sorts out the rules of language. She will also be able to talk about ideas as well as the concrete things around her. In this way, you can chat about anything from laziness to feelings to what would happen if we didn't have cars and buses.

Your child's vocabulary will continue to increase at a rapid rate and by the age of five she will be able to say at least 2000 words and will understand many more – in fact her questions will have become so sophisticated, it will be *you* who is struggling to find the right words with which to answer her.

Your three-year-old may have come home from nursery and tried to tell you that he did a finger painting. But he will appear to presume that you know something about it already and so will not give you quite enough information. For example, he may just say 'I used my fingers' and you will have to ask more questions before you fully understand what he has been doing. But by age four or five, your child is able to give you a fuller account of his activities, in chronological order and bearing in mind what you need to know. He will therefore now say something like 'We did a painting today and we used our fingers.' You can continue the conversation by expressing an interest and then following up with a question. You might, for example say 'How lovely, what colours did you use?' or 'I bet you enjoyed that. Did the teacher put it up on the wall?'

Before four years, your child will have been more self-centred, seeing things from her point of view only. But now this starts to change. Give a three-year-old two dolls and ask her to carry out the actions and she will have difficulty with sentences such as 'The boy kisses the girl' and is more likely to do the kissing herself. At three, she will feel it must be her doing the actions but this changes by the age of four when she will appreciate the importance of other people.

Your child will now use his language skills in different ways. There will be less talking to himself as he plays, although he will still 'talk himself through' a particularly demanding task. (But then, so do many adults!) Now he will be using language mainly to communicate to others – to tell other people what he needs and also to comment on what has been said to him. The conversations of four- and five-year-olds really are a two-way event, with each child listening to what the other has to say. Language will now be an aid to learning and discovery – if your child wants to know about something, he will ask. Talking will be used to make plans, to reason and to argue.

Talking has now become very inventive and creative so that by age five, your child will be able to make up her own stories, using her imagination as she does so. Even individual words and phrases can be inventive. A five-year-old once described a wall as being too 'edgery' when an adult would say 'narrow'. In this way, your child will not be restricted by her limited vocabulary – her language ability will enable her to say what she means, even if it is in a slightly unconventional way. You may find your child's stories are a mixture of fact and fantasy and for a while she may confuse the two. This will be a difficult age to get your child to stick to the truth – she won't always know what is fact and what is fiction!

More questions

You will still find yourself bombarded with questions but these should now become more relevant, with your child listening more carefully to the answer you give him. What, where, who, which, when, how and why questions will be asked as well as those made by changing the word order, for example, 'Are you going shopping?' or 'Is that for me?' Your child will also start to use tag questions – these are short questions tagged on to the end of a sentence, for example, 'You got my sweets, *didn't you?*' or 'I like this book, *don't I?*' He may make some errors with this to start with such as 'I can't have one, can't I?' and there will be errors with non-question tags such as 'You'd better do it, bettern you.' Your child may use the easier tags – 'Right?' and 'OK?' to start with, for example 'I'm watching television, right?' or 'I can play with this, OK?'

During this stage of putting quite complicated thoughts into words, your child's questions might just be thinking aloud. There may therefore be some occasions when your child is not always interested in your answers, or he may need your answers simply to confirm that his own thoughts or ideas are correct.

By age five, your child may be asking you quite complicated questions which are often a job to answer – 'How do ladybirds fly?', 'Where does air come from?' or 'Does the Queen like porridge?' – will all start off some interesting conversations. And it is at this stage that your child will gradually realise that you don't know everything! You will also be asked about the meaning of words and questions – 'What does "always" mean?' or 'What does "necessary" mean?' – which will improve your child's vocabulary but stretch your skills considerably. Just remember that giving examples – sentences containing the problem word – is always a good way of explaining. Don't assume that your child knows the meaning of something, just because she doesn't ask. You still need to ask her questions to make sure she has understood you.

Understanding and listening

Your child will now understand most of what is said to him and you won't have to simplify your own language to the same extent as you did when he was two or three. If he doesn't understand, he will quite often tell you or else ask questions, although there will still be a tendency to 'switch off' when something is too difficult to follow. Your child may well pay no attention when adults talk together in his presence, but there is no guarantee that he won't pick up the gist of what's being said. So be careful! His ears will certainly 'prick' up should he hear his name mentioned. Attention and listening skills will affect how much your child is understanding. He may have the underlying ability to understand but he won't be able to put it to good use if his mind is always wandering. Children with poor concentration do tend to have difficulty learning new things and this will affect their level of understanding.

By the age of five, your child should be able to play or carry out an activity and listen to your instructions at the same time. However, if the instructions are particularly complicated, then she will still need to stop what she's doing and give you her full attention, usually by looking at you.

There are still complex sentences which four- and five-year-olds clearly don't understand. Carol Chomsky carried out the well known experiment with a blindfolded doll. The majority of five-year-olds who were asked if the doll was easy to see or hard to see, replied that it was hard to see. When asked to make the doll easy to see, most of them took the blindfold off.

During this year, your child will begin to enjoy longer stories, often waiting in anticipation to find out what's going to happen next. He will be so sure about what is right in spoken language, that he will find anything 'wrong' extremely amusing. So your child will laugh at funny names and amusing nonsense words. He will enjoy silly stories about characters who go to school in a cardboard box wearing their pyjamas. Jokes and riddles, however, are not usually understood by four- and five-year-olds; they will probably laugh, but they won't know why they are laughing.

The sounds of speech

Your four-year-old should be easy to understand although a few immaturities of articulation remain. Most sounds will be pronounced correctly now but your child may still have difficulty with *th* and *r* and this is quite normal. Difficulty with some groups of sounds, such as *squ* or *str* is also common, so 'square' and 'string' may be pronounced 'skare' and 'sting'.

Your child still may have difficulty with longer words, with sounds being left out or sounds being made in the wrong order, for example, 'hopsital' and 'efelant'. When your child talks quickly, which she will often do in her eagerness to get the information out, sounds may also be swopped round between words – the classic example is 'par cark' for 'car park'.

Your child will be able to hear the difference between the correct and incorrect forms of all these 'errors', so if *you* make the same mistakes as she sometimes does, she will often be quick to point it out. She may be able to repeat the correct version after you. There is, of course, quite a variation from child to child – some children will have mastered all the sounds of speech by the time they start school, while others may still be having problems with a few sounds.

Family conversation

Your child can talk well enough to join in with some of the family conversations. He can give his opinion on where you go on holiday, what you have for dinner and what he wants to do next Sunday. But how often *is* there a family conversation in your house? How much opportunity does your child have to put his improved communication skills to good use? Does most of the 'conversation' in

STORIES AND QUESTIONS

your family consist of shouting out 'Dinner time!' or 'Turn that television off'? Or do you all sit down for a good chin-wag over breakfast each morning?

Consider the following questions and take a long, critical look at how much time each day is spent *really* talking to your child.

Is the television ever on when no one is watching it?

Is the radio ever on when no one is listening?

Do you ever try to engage your child in a conversation while the TV is on?

Does all the family sit down together at meal times?

Are your meal times generally very hurried?

Does your child have a quiet time at bedtime for looking at books with a parent and having a chat?

Do you ever sit and chat to your child while she's in the bath?

Do you try to involve your child in making some of the day-to-day decisions such as what to have for tea or what to wear?

Do you talk to your child about what you've been doing while he's been at playgroup?

If your child is not keen to talk about playgroup at first, do you try again later in the day?

Do you ever answer your child's questions with 'Because it just is', 'Because I say so' or 'Ask your father/mother'?

Do you *really* listen to your child, giving her your undivided attention, while she's telling you something that's important to her?

If you don't understand what your child is trying to tell you, do you ignore him or stick with it until you get the message?

Are your conversations a two-way exchange of ideas or is one of you asking the questions while the other answers quickly and briefly?

Do you enjoy chatting to your child?

Telephone time

Your child will have been fascinated by telephones from a very early age. Many babies not only have toy telephones but love picking up the real thing and babbling down it, even when there's no one at the other end. By the time your child is four or five, he will have progressed considerably. He will now have a complete understanding of exactly what the telephone is – that you can chat to people on it but they can't see you. By the age of five, your child should be able to answer the telephone competently and even take messages.

Teach your child how to answer the telephone, picking it up and saying nothing is useless. A clear, confident 'Hello' is probably the most effective. (It's not a good idea for your child to give her name, just in case the caller isn't bona fide.) When your child knows how to answer the telephone, let her answer it as often as possible. Allow her to make her own telephone call if, say, she wants to ask a friend to tea. Teach her how to introduce herself, for example, 'Hello, this is Jane Smith, may I speak to Judith please?'

Explain to your child why she shouldn't play with the telephone – she wouldn't be the first child to inadvertently phone Australia! Take a trip to the local telephone box and show your child how it works. This will reinforce the idea, early on, that telephone calls cost money. Show your child how to dial 999 and explain when and why this might be necessary. Make sure she knows her address.

Parents can enjoy telephoning their children when they are away. If your child is used to talking on the phone, he is less likely to 'clam up'. Talking without seeing the listener is a different experience from talking face to face and your child will need to get used to it.

At a glance: what your four-and-a-half-year-old can do

- Use sentences of four, five or six words – sometimes even longer.
- Have a large vocabulary, often of several thousand words.
- Use sentences which are, on the whole, grammatically correct, though some 'mistakes' will still be heard from time to time.
- Count up to twenty but with little understanding. Count objects or pictures up to four or five.
- Give you detailed accounts of what she has been doing in your absence.
- Ask endless questions.
- Tell familiar stories and make up her own.
- Recite and sing nursery rhymes.
- Begin to take an active part in family conversations.

Talking to your four- to five-year-old

Your child will be leading a busy life now and won't always feel like talking. Do allow her to be quiet and to have some privacy when she needs it. Get to know your child, take note of whether she switches off if you talk in complicated sentences and change your speaking accordingly. But don't simplify things too much – your child will be learning new words and sentences all the time. And she'll be learning them from you.

If your child is a confident talker at home, he will find it easier to talk outside the home. So give your child plenty of opportunities for chat. Don't just expect him to 'perform' in public. If your child tells you something interesting, praise him. He needs encouragement and the reward of you saying 'That's interesting' or 'I do like talking to you.'

In this year before school, ensure that your child has an interest in books. Read her a story each day, join the library and let her see *you* reading books for pleasure. Start a diary or scrap book and write in it when you do something special. Your child can help by sticking in tickets or lolly wrappers from the day. Then, when she visits grandparents or friends, she can take it with her so that they have something to talk about.

Whenever possible, give your child your full attention when he's talking to you and make sure he is listening properly when you are talking to him. Remember that what may seem trivial to you, might be of utmost importance to your child so give him your attention whatever the subject. Try not to laugh when your child makes mistakes or gets things wrong. Sometimes you can laugh *with* him, but laughing at him may put him off talking.

As your child approaches school age, make sure you occasionally use words which are new to her. Explain what each new word means and repeat it in different conversations over two or three days. Don't worry about correcting your child's grammar – just make sure she hears the correct form from you soon after the mistake. For example, she may say 'I buyed some sweets' and you may say 'Yes, you *bought* two packets of sweets, didn't you.'

Games and activities

I went to market

A good game for helping with listening and memory (both essential skills for learning language). You can play this just with your child, with the whole family or with a group of children. You start by saying 'I went to market and I bought ____ (name an object)'. Your child then repeats 'I went to market and I bought a ____ (your object) and ____' (adds another one). The list then gets longer and you each have to keep remembering all the items. Your four- or five-year-old will do well to remember four items.

STORIES AND QUESTIONS

Kim's game

Another good memory game, this time using memory for what we see, rather than what we hear. Put out a tray of objects for your child and her friends to look at. Take the tray out of sight and remove one item. Now see if your child can work out what you have taken away. Start with a choice of three objects and gradually increase the number (and the time given to study the tray). Increase your child's vocabulary by including unusual items which she may not know the name of.

Draw-as-your-told

This is a good exercise in using language precisely and in finding the right words. Give your child a simple picture, perhaps a blue circle with a red dot in the middle. He must then give the right instructions to an adult or another child to enable that person to draw it correctly, without seeing the original picture.

Concept snap

Try this with your five-year-old. The pictures in this snap game are all different but 'snap' can be called if there is a link between the two pictures – it may be that they are both animals, or both used in the kitchen or even both breakable. A clear reason for saying snap must be given. Your child may find this game difficult to start with but once she gets the idea, she will enjoy it. Use ordinary picture snap games – perhaps mixing two different sets together – or make your own by cutting out magazine pictures and sticking them on to card.

Listening stories

This will encourage your child to listen to each part of the story with no chance of switching off. Start with an animal story and tell your child to make the appropriate noise every time you mention the name of an animal. Then collect a group of objects or toys together and tell a story about a birthday or Christmas. Every time a present is mentioned, your child must go and fetch it from the pile of items you have collected.

Shops

Children of this age love playing shops, particularly with their friends. Start them off by being a customer in the shop, asking some awkward questions. Try 'Have you got something for breakfast that will fit into my bag?', 'Have you got a suitable present for a baby boy?' or 'Have you got something to take on holiday?' Encourage the children to use lots of talk in this way as they play, and get them to discuss together how they are going to set up the shop. All you need to provide are a lot of old packets and cartons.

Board games

These are excellent for helping your child to take turns and to pay attention to simple rules. 'Snakes and ladders' is an old favourite and there are many other 'track' games available which are suitable for this age group. You could also help your child make a board game of his own and this will obviously involve a good deal of discussion. Start by drawing a simple track of squares to move round and see if your child can come up with a set of rules such as 'If you land on a red square, you go back to the beginning.' After you've played it, you can discuss together whether it's a good game and what other rules could be added.

Which way are you going?

Many children of this age group enjoy playing with cars and trains, but do not talk very much apart from saying 'broom broom' and other such noises. Vehicles with people who get in and out are more likely to get a conversation going, but another idea is to draw a layout of streets on to a large piece of paper. Your child can then help to draw on the buildings, trees, zebra crossings etc. Then take turns at giving each other directions for moving your car along. You might say 'Go along the main road, past the school and park in the car park by the bank' or 'Go along the main road, stop at the zebra crossing and park outside the Post Office'. This provides a good opportunity to introduce the idea of left and right.

Song tapes and story tapes

Television requires less listening and attention than stories on a tape-recorder. A child can watch the action on TV without really listening to or being aware of the story. Story tapes with an accompanying book (your child doesn't have to be able to read) are good for building up concentration skills. These can be bought but it's a good idea to make your own. This way you can start with a fairly short and simple story and gradually build up to longer ones. Simply choose your child's favourite book and record you reading it into a tape-recorder. Each time the page needs to be turned, record a sound such as a bell ringing or simply say 'Turn the page'. Song tapes are also useful – encourage your child to sing along and turn down the sound occasionally to see if she can remember the words on her own.

Questions … questions … questions …

> ❛ My child was late starting to talk – he was two before
> he said any words at all. He's now a happy
> four-year-old who talks in sentences but he still
> doesn't talk quite as well as his friends of the
> same age. Will he always be a poor speaker? ❜

Children who are late starting to talk will need time to 'catch up'. And a child who has only been speaking for two years may well have more immature language than a child who has been speaking for nearly three. He does need extra time but he also needs just that little extra input from you to ensure that his communication

TALKING AND YOUR CHILD

skills continue to develop. Set aside a time each day for playing with your child, choosing toys which will involve a lot of chat between you – a farm set, doll's house or perhaps puppets. In your special play sessions, ask your child different types of questions – 'Which animal shall we put in the field?', 'Where shall we put the pig?', 'How can we fit the man into the tractor?' and 'When do you want to stop for a drink?' If he finds listening to your instructions difficult, then get his attention first, making sure that he looks at you while you are speaking. Give your child varied instructions as well such as 'Put the man next to the pig', 'Put all the sheep in the field' etc. This may seem as though you are doing all the talking but it is by listening to you that he will learn good language skills.

> ❝ My child never stops talking at home but as soon as we see a neighbour in the street, she either hides behind my skirt or talks in a babyish voice. ❞

This is quite common – some children are more confident than others and confidence, or lack of it, obviously affects communication skills. Accept your child's personality if she is shy and never criticise her for this. Instead, concentrate on praising her when she does talk confidently even if, to start with, this is in the confines of your own home. If your child becomes shy in public, just ignore it and carry on talking yourself. When she comes out from behind you, try to include her in the conversation. Children who feel under stress or threatened in some way often regress to a babyish voice and this is best ignored. Just ensure that you are not putting her under pressure to 'perform' in public. Pay attention to what your child is saying rather than how she is saying it and she will soon outgrow this stage. Make sure she has plenty of opportunity for meeting and talking to different people. Take her to play with other children and to a playgroup or nursery.

> ❝ My child doesn't listen. On some occasions, I know he's heard me for although I don't get an immediate response, he will suddenly reply or do what he's been asked about half an hour later. ❞

STORIES AND QUESTIONS

Your child may still be at the stage when you need to get him to look you in the eyes and stop what he's been doing before you know he's paying attention. Do this by calling his name and then maintain eye contact while you talk. It may help to switch off the television or any other background noises. Your child may benefit from games which will help him to listen and to pay attention – Simon says, Chinese whispers or even musical bumps are good ones so perhaps you should have an impromptu party. A delayed response is very common but do make sure that your child has plenty of opportunities to have real conversations with you and that your communications between each other are more than just giving one another instructions or making demands.

> **My four-and-a-half-year-old cannot say his 'th's and 'r's. He says 'woad' for 'road' and 'fum' for 'thumb'. Is he lazy?**

It is quite normal for children up to the age of six or seven to have difficulty with these sounds. He is not being lazy – his speech is perfectly normal for a child of this age. Just make sure he is always hearing the right version from you without correcting him as such. So, for example, if he says 'My fum hurts', you might reply 'Oh dear, what happened to your *thumb*?' You could also try playing a listening game where you say words in a story incorrectly and your child gets a point for every one he spots. Include words like 'woad' and 'fum' as well as other, perhaps easier, mistakes.

CHAPTER SEVEN

At home and school (five to seven years)

By the time your child starts school, you will be confident that she can now really talk. You will feel able to talk to her as an equal, that she understands everything you say and that she can say whatever she wants to whoever she wants. Immaturities and lack of the right words no longer hold her back. However, is her language fully developed? Does she really speak like an adult would? When you listen to your five-year-old chatting and arguing with friends you may be left wondering what there is left to learn, but children's language continues to change and develop until they are well into their teens. The changes may be less dramatic than those of a one-year-old learning her first words, but nevertheless there will be developments, however subtle.

The main change is not so much the new words and sentences your child can use, but the fact that she can say her existing words and sentences better. Most of her grammatical mistakes will disappear during the first couple of years at school, as will errors with the sounds of speech.

'I've got a bike and a car and a pram and a scooter and . . .'

Your child will also start to use a wider variety of 'linking' words. A four-year-old tends to link his ideas almost entirely with 'and' –

'We went to the shops and we bought some sweets and we came home on the bus and I am hungry and I want some now.' A five- or six-year-old can link ideas in different ways, making his talk sound altogether more mature – 'We went to the shops *to* buy some sweets, *then* we came home on the bus. I feel hungry *so* can I have some now?'

'I'm 5, actually'

Your child's vocabulary will increase, particularly after starting school when a whole range of new ideas and words will come into her life. This, in turn, will help to make her conversations sound more mature, particularly when she starts using adult-sounding words such as 'actually', 'probably' and 'in fact'. She will also become adept at using 'if' sentences – 'If it rains, then we can't go to the playground.'

Speech sounds

By age seven, your child should have mastered all the sounds of speech. If there are still ongoing difficulties with *r* and *th*, these may follow him into adulthood.

What your child understands

Your child will appear to understand everything you say, with the exception of more complex and specialised words. Provided you can get her to listen, she will respond to all your requests and instructions. It's really only when you get down to some of the finer details of language that you will find there are some limitations as to what five- to seven-year-olds understand.

Man bites dog

Children of this age assume that the first person or item in the sentence is doing the action. This is normally the case in standard sentences such as 'The dog is biting the man' or 'Daddy rides the horse.' But more complex sentences such as 'The girl was hit by the boy', where the second person is doing the action, are more difficult for children of this age to understand. It would appear to a five-year-old, that the girl is doing the hitting. Obviously, in many instances, common sense will help your child understand sentences like this. 'The man was bitten by a dog' is less likely to be misunderstood by your child because she knows that a dog is more likely to be doing the biting. Of course, word order in sentences can get even more complicated – 'The man the dog bit was playing golf' or 'The baby the mother was holding clapped her hands' would be very difficult for children of this age to sort out.

An experiment was carried out in 1974 by two psychologists (Carbon and Sinclair) which clearly demonstrated how five-year-olds rely on word order to tell them who is doing the action. They gave a group of five-year-olds a doll and asked them to carry out certain actions. When the children were given a sentence such as 'The doll is easy to draw', they made the doll do the drawing.

Ask and tell

Carol Chomsky found that children of this age group have difficulty understanding the difference between 'ask' and 'tell'. You can check this with your own child by sending her to take a message. If you say 'Ask Daddy if he wants Spaghetti for supper', you may find your child informing him that spaghetti *is* for supper. She has *told* him, not *asked* him. If you say 'Ask Daddy what colour this box is', she may go straight to him and tell him that the box is blue.

Off to school

Good effects on talking

Your child will suddenly be bombarded with new ideas, new information and new situations. His vocabulary and understanding are bound to improve. As he cannot rely on adults he knows to anticipate his needs, he will have to communicate well in order to ask for and get what he wants. He will be using his language skills to build up relationships with teachers and other children.

If you have moved to a different area, your child will adopt the local accent, if he hasn't already done so. Some parents may consider this as being a 'bad effect' but don't correct him – he's simply becoming integrated into his community which is no bad thing. Anyway, you won't be able to do much about it!

Your child will be encouraged to talk about home to his teacher and friends. There may be a 'news time' to give the children confidence in speaking out.

Bad effects on talking

Your child may 'pick up' a different way of speaking depending who she chooses to play with – 'Yea', 'Naah' and slang words may suddenly appear. Do not blame particular children, as this is a form of group behaviour which your child will have to learn to confine to when she's with friends.

Your child may seem to go backwards when she first starts school. It's a big step and may bring out a shy and non-communicative side to her. Give her a chance to settle in before you expect to hear much about what she's done all day.

You may find yourself spending time practising reading or number work at home. But remember, your child still needs plenty of time to talk to you. A quiet story and chat at the end of the day is as important as ever.

Games and activities

Charades

Take it in turns to act out an everyday activity. Good actions to mime are washing up, making the bed, cleaning the car, washing your hair, putting on shoes etc. Then introduce activities to mime which involve acting out a sequence of actions in the right order. For example, going to school would involve putting on a coat, getting in the car or bus, hanging up a coat on the peg etc. Ask a group of six- and seven-year-olds to mime the name of a television programme for adults to guess. Encourage the children to discuss their mime together before they perform it.

Story circles

Play this with one or more children. Begin to tell a story then stop at an interesting point and let your child carry on. If your child finds this difficult, start by re-telling a familiar story with your child filling in parts of it. Then try to encourage your child to use language creatively and imaginatively by making up a completely new story. Children love stories about themselves, so you could start off with something like 'One day, Jane opened up her toy cupboard when out fell . . .' At first she may only fill in one or two words, but once she gets the idea, she will say a couple of sentences and after a while, you won't be able to stop her.

What would happen if . . .

Give your child some teasing questions to think about – 'What would happen if all the cars were yellow?' 'What would happen if we only had one arm each?' or 'What would happen if we had no paper?' Get your child to think of some to ask you.

Treasure hunt

Make up a set of clues (about seven) for your child to solve. Once he has solved a clue, he gains a token, and once he has collected all the tokens he gets the clue for the main 'treasure' – perhaps a packet of sweets or, at the right time of year, an Easter egg. Give your child increasingly complex clues as to where the 'treasure' may be hidden. Clues could range from 'Look amongst the flowers immediately in front of the house' to 'Find something that blooms in the spring near to the place where you come in.' When your child has solved one clue, she comes to you to hear another. This is a good party game.

Twenty questions

Six- and seven-year-olds can start to enjoy a simple version of this game. You choose an item and your child has to guess what it is by asking questions. You can only reply with 'Yes' or 'No'. To start with, you could restrict it by choosing an object in the room and then extend it to some item in the house. At first, your child may ask some very narrow questions along the lines of 'Is it a table?' or 'Is it a chair?' However, if you take a turn at guessing an object your child has thought of, then he will hear the sort of useful questions that you ask – 'Do we use it every day?' 'Is it smaller than a cup?' etc.

What's the difference?

These activities are very good for five-year-olds and can be found in puzzle books or you can draw your own. You need two pictures which are identical except for one or two small differences which your child has to spot. But get her to *tell* you what the difference is rather than point to it. She will therefore have to use precise and sometimes quite complex sentences – 'That elephant has got a smaller ear on that side' or 'That elephant has one tusk slightly higher than the other' etc.

Build it like me

Give yourself and your child an identical set of bricks and then sit out of each other's sight but within hearing distance. You then build a 'house' giving your child precise instructions as you go, such as 'Put the little blue brick on to the large red one.' You should end up with two identical constructions if your child has listened carefully. Now swap roles and let your child give you the instructions. Two children can play this game together.

Mini-plays

Your child will now enjoy acting out a familiar story with friends. Parents provide the applause in their role as the audience. Most of the talk will actually take place during the preparation when the children will be deciding who is going to do what and roughly what they are going to say. Keep things simple at first by suggesting a story they all know well such as 'The Three Bears' or 'Little Red Riding Hood'.

Blindfold obstacle course

Your child must give you or another child instructions for going round a pre-set obstacle course. The difficulty lies in the fact that you are blindfolded and rely solely on clear, precise instructions from your child to get through the course. Make sure that there are plenty of obstacles to go over, through, under or round and that the blindfolded person needs to steer to the right or left. Respond to the instructions exactly as they are given. This is a good game for using language precisely and accurately. Another version is for your child to give you instructions for moving a toy car or small doll round a mini-obstacle course.

Word association

You start the game off by saying any word you like. Then each player has to follow on with an associated word without hesitating or repeating a word which has already been said. You will find that younger children will say a word which 'goes' with the previous word, for example, if you say 'black' she may say 'cat' and if you say 'blue' she may say 'sky'. An older child, on the other hand, will look at words in terms of the group they belong to and is more likely to say the name of another colour.

Questions ... questions ... questions ...

‘ My child spends a lot of time watching television. I
don't mind him watching educational programmes as
these will improve his knowledge and vocabulary,
but he usually watches cartoons. Surely he can't
learn much from these? ’

Television has more than one function. On the one hand, children
do learn a lot from it – they see animals, countries and events
which they may not have the opportunity of seeing otherwise, and
they will be learning from what they hear and see. On the other
hand, television is also a means of entertainment and relaxation.
Adults use the TV more for entertainment than for education, so
perhaps we shouldn't expect our children to be any different. Just
watch out for endless TV watching, particularly when it involves
your child simply sitting in front of programme after programme
without really listening at all. Your child can gain a lot from watching entertainment programmes – even watching cartoons involves
listening and concentration – but if your child can't tell you what
the programme was about afterwards, it may be time to reach for
the off switch.

Your child may unwind in front of the television after a hard
day at school and there may be times for allowing this. However,
it may be worth teaching your child to be selective about the
programmes he watches and to find some other way of unwinding.
Discussing his choice of programmes is a good opportunity for
conversation in itself. You could read through the options
together, talking about which programmes look good and sel-
ecting one or two to watch. It's also a good idea to watch a
programme with your child from time to time and then you can
talk about it afterwards.

TALKING AND YOUR CHILD

❝ My child used to speak precisely and clearly. Since
starting school, all we hear is 'yea' and 'naah',
slang and sloppy speech. Should we correct him
or will he grow out of it? ❞

Your child will probably always have a different way of speaking
with his friends, just as we might speak in a different manner to
our boss as compared with how we speak to a neighbour. Learning
to adjust the way he speaks to suit the situation is a subtle art which
will take your child a while to accomplish. So rather than tell your
child off point blank for the words he is using or how he's saying
them, point out that it is all right to speak like that in the playground
but not at home. Some parents accept slang in the home but teach
their children that it is not acceptable in front of guests or out in
public. It is up to you to set your own rules over what is acceptable.
Just make sure that your child is clear about these rules and that
you and your partner are consistent in the way you deal with slang.
Encouraging enthusiasm for conversation is still more important, so
when your child rushes home from school with some interesting
news to tell you, it is probably better to show your interest in his
news before butting in with an automatic 'Do you have to speak
like that?'

❝ My child now knows and uses several swear words.
If I make a fuss, I'm sure she'll do it even more
but how can I ignore it? ❞

This problem tends to occur once a child has started school. It is
important to ensure that your child knows that some words are
unacceptable – she might not realise just quite how unacceptable
they are if she has simply copied them from an older child in the
playground. Just quietly and calmly explain that we do not use the
particular word as it is rude, and that adults would think badly of
a child who did use such words. With older children, you might
point out that swearing is only acceptable amongst friends and not
in front of adults – but this would depend on your personal point

AT HOME AND SCHOOL

of view. Some children swear in order to get your attention. In this instance, it is best ignored to show your child that it really doesn't get any attention at all. At the same time, though, it is important to think about why your child is seeking extra attention in this way. Perhaps she is not getting enough response when she is talking politely, so ensure that she gets your undivided attention when she is telling you something interesting, ignoring any further bad language.

(*My child seems to have a very limited vocabulary. He talks very well for his age but surprises me with the words he doesn't know. How can I help?*)

Children of school age are still building up their vocabulary (the number of words they use and understand) and are continuously learning new words both at home and at school. Children certainly learn new words and ideas from books, and if parents stop reading bedtime stories to their children, preferring the child to do the reading, it may be that they are not hearing a wide enough vocabulary. Early reading books have only limited vocabulary and sentence structures, so do read a story to your child each day and don't always rely on books with pictures – your child should be able to listen well now. Make sure you explain any words which your child might not have come across before. Go on walks and outings and watch television together. Your child will learn new words from new experiences. Once your child can read well, encourage him to read for pleasure – go to the library regularly and take out both fiction and non-fiction books. And don't forget to take out books for yourself too. If your child sees you reading for pleasure, he won't need much convincing that reading is indeed pleasurable. When a new word does come up in a story or in conversation, reinforce your child's understanding of the word by trying to bring it into further conversations.

CHAPTER EIGHT

Letters and laughter (seven to ten years)

By the time your child is seven or eight, it will be difficult to find many differences between her talk and that of an adult. Her vocabulary may be smaller, because most adults will have had wider experiences in life, and the topics she chooses to talk about may be altogether different, but the structure of her speech will be very similar. Your child's language will now take on many of the sophisticated niceties of an adult – she will have progressed from a three-year-old saying 'Put the tele on now' to, hopefully, a more mature 'Can I put the television on?' Even 'I'm putting the tele on whether you like it or not' has a very sophisticated structure and sound to it, even if the tone is not to your liking. Given the experience, your child can talk about anything and can incorporate adult-like subtleties into her conversations, whether she's dropping hints or using humour – both complex uses of language.

Your worries about your child's communication skills will suddenly change. You will no longer be concerned that the boy next door talks more than your child or that your child is slow at speaking. Late starters should have caught up by now and you will be more anxious about other aspects of communication, such as talking politely or talking confidently. During this period, you will also move on from worrying about whether your child will ever tell you about his activities at playgroup to whether your child can talk easily with you about his fears and problems. If you have always had time for a chat during the early years when your child's language was developing, then hopefully you will continue to give your child this time.

Earlier, you may have been inundated with awkward questions such as 'What does "popular" mean', stretching your own communication skills considerably. Now it will be the subject matter which may stretch you as you find yourself answering questions about everything, from where babies come from to why Auntie Janet is getting divorced. Always check that you understand your child's question before launching into complicated and intimate answers. One child asked what incest meant. Her mother, surprised by the question, asked her where she had heard such a word. The child replied 'Don't you incest on Walkers crisps!'

Dear Sur or Madman

During this time, your child will develop another means of communication – writing. Initially, this will be seen as 'work' carried out at school. But you can help reinforce the fact that writing is really another way of 'talking'.

- Set an example. Let your child see you write letters to your friends and relatives and talk about the letters you receive in the post – even if it is just from the bank manager!
- Help your child to send postcards to her friends when you go on holiday.
- Let your child help with day-to-day writing tasks such as compiling the shopping list or putting out a note for the milkman.
- Leave notes around the house for your child to read. For example, pin a note on the fridge saying 'Please don't touch the strawberries before tea' or leave a letter on his bed saying 'Thank you for tidying your room – it looks perfect.'
- As your child gets older, encourage her to write creatively.

Write stories and poems together and pin the best ones up on the wall for the whole family to read.

You must be joking

One of the most sophisticated uses of language must be telling jokes. Not the custard-pie-in-the-face type of joke which even three-year-olds find funny, but the play on words which requires a good vocabulary and reasonable level of understanding. Five-year-olds may well laugh at 'school-boy' puns and 'knock-knock' jokes, but this is usually just social laughter and they don't usually know why the joke is funny.

Try telling your child a meaningless joke such as 'Why did the chicken cross the road? – To jump on a kangaroo' and you will get the same social laughter. (You may even find that your child makes up her own jokes with the right question and answer format but with no actual joke in it.) It won't be until your child is about seven, that she will say 'Don't get it' or 'That's not funny.'

Take the following jokes:

What is a crocodile's favourite game? – Snap.
Why is a pony like someone with a sore throat? – Because they are both a little hoarse.
What sort of crisps fly? – Plain crisps.

To appreciate jokes like these, your child needs to understand that one word can have more than one meaning.

Knock knock; Who's there? Gorilla. Gorilla who? Gorilla piece of bacon.
Knock knock; Who's there? Freddie. Freddie who? Freddie, steady, go.

For these, your child needs to appreciate that some words sound similar to, or rhyme with, other words.

What kind of animal can jump higher than a house? Any animal – houses can't jump.

Is it better to write on a full or an empty stomach? Neither – paper is much better.

These require a feel for the ambiguity of sentences – again quite a sophisticated view of language.

What goes clomp clomp squish, clomp clomp squish? – An elephant with a wet shoe.

What goes 99 bonk, 99 bonk? A centipede with a wooden leg.

These merely require a sense of the ridiculous.

Your child needs to have a certain level of knowledge to appreciate some jokes. For instance, the '99 bonk' joke is only funny if you already know that centipedes have 100 legs. Of course, none of these jokes are really funny to us, but when we groan, our children laugh. And take a deep breath, for once your child starts to appreciate these so-called jokes, they will tell them incessantly – and this stage can go on for several years!

Playing with language

Jokes and puns are really just a way of playing with words and your child may well start to play with language in other ways. In the playground, for example, you will hear children trying to invent their own secret language, usually based on ours, but incorporating some trick to stop unwanted listeners from understanding what is being said. One popular idea is putting a sound such as 'og' before every vowel so that 'table' would be pronounced 'togabloge'. Another common idea is saying words backwards which requires skill and a good deal of practice.

At the same time, your child will be learning about language at school. Many schools will be teaching your child about the basics of grammar and defining words such as 'vowel' and 'consonant'. All this is good preparation for when your child moves on from making up her own language in the playground to learning a foreign language such as French or German.

Games and activities

The following games can all be played with a group of children or with the family. While you are all enjoying yourselves, your child will be learning, without even realising it. So have fun with these activities and think up some of your own.

Just a minute

This popular radio quiz can be adapted for playing at home. Each player has to try and speak for one minute on a subject chosen by the others. Perhaps, to start with, your child could choose her own topic. Repetitions of any kind are not allowed, so if the speaker uses the same word twice, he can be challenged by another player who then carries on until the minute is up.

Yes and no quiz

One player questions another for one or two minutes. The player answering is not allowed to say 'yes' or 'no' and the questioner must try and catch him out. Let your child have a turn at both roles.

Call my bluff

This is just like the popular television team game, although it can be played with just two people. One player finds an obscure word in the dictionary and then gives three definitions of the word, one of which is the correct one. The other player then has to choose the right definition. To start with, the adult will probably give the definitions with the child choosing. This could therefore be used as a way of building up your child's vocabulary, in which case the words you choose won't be that obscure. Check to see whether your child has remembered what the words mean afterwards.

Doing the opposite

A good group or party game which will even catch out some adults. An adult shouts out instructions and everyone else has to do the opposite of that command. Start with simple commands such as 'Stand up' (everyone must sit down) or 'Move to the right' (everyone must move to the left). Gradually introduce longer, more complicated instructions such as 'Stand up with your eyes open' (everyone must sit down with their eyes shut) or 'Turn to the left, put your right hand out and walk in a straight line while you laugh' (everyone gets in a right muddle).

Remember this!

Discuss with the children a series of instructions which will have a code word, such as a colour. For example, red might mean 'touch the floor', green could mean 'run to the table', yellow might mean 'turn round in a circle' etc. Then just shout out a colour. The players must remember what action to carry out in response to the colour. Later you can shout out more than one colour for your child to carry out a sequence of actions, and you can gradually add more colours and corresponding actions. Once the children start to remember the instructions easily, swop all the colours round. In other words, if red had previously meant 'touch the floor', change it so that green means 'touch the floor' and red means 'run to the table'.

Brainy box-watchers

If your child is on the verge of becoming a TV addict and if you are on the verge of throwing something rather heavy at the off switch, here are three activities centred around the curse of the sitting room – the tele.

1 TV commentaries

Turn the sound down while your child is watching an event or favourite sport and let him do the commentary. This is more difficult than it sounds and it definitely requires careful watching and concentration, which your child might not normally have while watching cricket for two hours on a Saturday afternoon.

2 TV reviews
Encourage your child to have opinions about the programmes she watches and help her to express them constructively. To begin with, you might get little more than 'It's great' or 'That's rubbish', but discussing programmes with her afterwards should help to expand her views. Read out some of the reviews in the newspaper and talk about whether you agree with them or not.

3 Home TV station
Cut out the shape of a TV from a large cardboard box and get your child to draw the knobs. There should be a square hole in the middle so that when a child sits behind it, it looks like he's on television. Children can then take it in turns to read the news, forecast the weather and so on. You can take this simple activity a step further by getting your child to interview other children and adults. The other children could take on the role of a famous person to add a touch of imagination to the game.

Listen here

Play any games which encourage good listening skills – from Chinese whispers to listening to story tapes. You can also have quiet times when you ask your child or a group of children to keep exceptionally quiet and then say, or write down, what they can hear. In the house, this might be the buzz of the fridge or a tap dripping, and outside they may hear the rustling of leaves. Ask your child to describe what the noises sound like and you should hear some imaginative and descriptive language. A good time to do this is first thing in the morning, so when your child goes to bed at night remind her to listen carefully when she wakes up and to remember the first three sounds she hears.

LETTERS AND LAUGHTER

Creative thinking

Encourage your child to use her language creatively and thought-fully. When you are out for a walk or on an outing, you could discuss what things look like. For example, ask him what the washing on the line looks like and put in a few of your own ideas – perhaps it looks like flowers in the breeze or flags on a castle. Similarly, discuss what the dead leaves *sound* like as you walk through them, what dew-covered cobwebs *look* like and what the long wet grass *feels* like as you walk through it. You may find that your child has quite a strong imagination and just needs a little encouragement to verbalise it.

Questions ... questions ... questions ...

❨ My daughter talks well and a lot! She chats about most things to everyone, including me. But when she has a problem, she just shuts herself in her room and doesn't communicate at all. **❩**

Once your child *can* talk well, it's rather up to her to decide *when* she talks and *what* she talks about. Remember that children will handle problems in different ways – some may run to Mum or Dad and cry on their shoulder while others may need time on their own. The important thing is that your child feels she *can* talk to you if she wants to and that she will get a sympathetic ear when it's needed rather than immediate cries of 'It's your own fault' or 'I told you so.' Firstly, make sure that your child has the opportunity to talk to you. Try to make sure that there is a quiet time each day set aside for just that purpose, and if there is an occasion when you feel that there is something troubling her, you could try a gentle but unpressurised 'Is there anything worrying you?' Secondly, make sure that your communications with your child are not all reprimands and laying down rules. If she is used to talking to you as an equal, she may feel more ready to talk about problems. And thirdly, make sure that you really do listen when your child discusses a worry. If the problem involves the fact that your child has done something wrong, it's all too easy to jump down her throat with an angry reprimand. This isn't going to help your child sort out her worry and is likely to stop her talking to you about a problem on future occasions. If a telling-off is needed, then save it until the problem has been discussed and you are both feeling calm.

> *My child has a hoarse voice. I'm sure it's because she's always shouting – she doesn't seem able to talk at a normal level.*

There are many causes of a hoarse voice – the most obvious occurring along with a bad cold. Usually once the infection clears up the voice improves. However, if the hoarse voice continues, then further investigation is needed and your first step should be to ask your doctor for a referral to an ear, nose and throat specialist who will check your child's vocal cords. If your child shouts a lot then you may need to get her hearing checked. If all seems well with her general health and hearing, your child is probably misusing her voice – she has got into the habit of shouting and may be forcing her voice out, perhaps with a poor breathing pattern. This may ultimately cause a physical problem with the vocal cords. Ask for a referral to a speech and language therapist who will help your child to use her voice correctly and liaise with the ear, nose and throat clinic if necessary.

> *They don't seem to teach good grammar in school these days, either spoken or written. Is there anything I can do to help at home?*

Grammar is certainly still taught in schools but not in the same way as we were taught. Rigid learning of rules has been dropped in favour of a more practical look at grammar as we use it. To help at home, you could introduce grammatical rules in a practical way, discussing them as you use them. For example, your child might

LETTERS AND LAUGHTER

say 'You're not never going to take none of my sweets again!' This has clearly broken the rule of not using more than one negative in a sentence (not, never and none) but rather than teach your child the rule with a definition of what a negative is, you could discuss together the different ways of saying the same thing. Point out *why* three negatives are unnecessary and get her to hear the difference between her sentence and a more correctly formed sentence.

Always provide your child with a good model by using correct grammar yourself and by reading books to her as well as encouraging her to read herself. When poor grammar occurs on television or in pop songs, use it as a point of discussion rather than condemning it immediately. After all, it may be your child's heroes you are criticising!

> ❝ My child doesn't *always* use the correct word for things, preferring to use new words and phrases that he has picked up from the television or from pop singers. How can I get him to stick to words from the dictionary? ❞

Remember that language changes all the time. We don't have the same vocabulary or grammar today as they did, say, 100 years ago. And just look at the writing of Shakespeare – it's positively difficult to follow at times because our language has changed so much. Every year, new words come into common usage and are therefore added to the dictionary. Even the word 'perfick' was recently considered for the dictionary following its use in a TV adaptation of *The Darling Buds of May* by H. E. Bates. 'Cowabunga' has similarly been considered after its hero turtle connections. Of course, some new words simply come about because of new inventions – computer-based words now in common usage were rarely heard thirty years ago.

Language certainly tends to be less formal these days and your child's talk will reflect this change. So try to avoid looking at new words as either correct or incorrect. Instead, emphasise the need for your child's language to be appropriate to the situation. 'Cowabunga' may find its way into the dictionary but, as yet, would hardly be an appropriate word to use at an interview with the headteacher.

CHAPTER NINE

Difficulties and differences

Why some children speak earlier and better than others

It is always dangerous to compare your child's language development with that of your friend's child or the child down the road. Sooner or later you will come across a child of exactly the same age who talks as if he could present a current affairs programme on television while your child is happily babbling to her soft toys. You will then find yourself worrying in case your child is backward in some way when the week before you had been so proud of all her new noises. But for your comparison to be in any way valid, the other child would need to be exactly the same age (even three months can make the world of difference), the same sex, the same position in the family and have the same experiences and hereditary factors. In other words, they would need to be twins before the comparison would be at all fair. Of course, all parents worry in case their children might be slow or have learning problems, and talking would seem to be a clue to general ability. But remember, your child is progressing in other areas as well. Perhaps she has a good memory or very mature visual skills; perhaps she is physically very able or is showing signs of independence with her new self-help skills.

Although there is much you can do to help your child on her way, she will develop at her own rate. So enjoy her development and concentrate on comparing your child's talking with how she was talking last month or last year rather than with how her cousin is talking. Some children will start to talk very early while others will take longer to progress – the reason isn't always obvious but do consider the following nine factors which have an effect on language development:

1 Just to be different

Perhaps the main reason for the variations in children's language development is that we are all different. It would be a strange and somewhat dull world if all our children said their first words at the age of twelve months and fourteen days. It would be odd if all four-year-olds knew the meaning of exactly the same amount of words, or if all our six-year-olds chatted to us about the same things. The main thing is to be careful that you don't interpret these differences as meaning that one child is in some way better than the next.

There is, as with all aspects of child development, an hereditary factor involved. This is only small, but if you or other members of your family were slow at starting to talk, then this could account for your child's late development. If you are worried, it may be worth talking to your own parents and your in-laws about how you both talked as young children. If you are an eldest child, your mother may well remember the exact time you said your first word or sentence. If you are a third or fourth child, then don't be surprised if the memories are a little more vague!

2 What parents do

This is a very important cause of variation. Children learn how to talk from listening to adults and older children close to them, particularly their parents. It therefore goes without saying that if you don't talk to your children, then they won't learn to talk. Of

DIFFICULTIES AND DIFFERENCES

course, it is only in extreme cases that a child is ever deprived of hearing language at all. One such case was Jeannie, a thirteen-year-old girl who had been kept in a room on her own in Los Angeles. No one spoke to her and if she made any noise, she was punished. She didn't learn to talk until she was found and fostered out and even then, she never really acquired normal grammatical speech. Profoundly deaf children are also deprived of hearing their parents talk and won't therefore learn to communicate as readily as hearing children, although lip reading and sign language will help them catch up.

Normal children in ordinary families will hear a variety of talk going on around them. It has been shown that the quantity and quality of that talk will affect their own speech and language development. Talking to your child as much as possible is one thing, but making sure that your talking is appropriate for your child's age, is interesting and that your child has a chance to communicate back to you are also important factors. Parents who put a real emphasis on communication and who are aware of their role in teaching and encouraging their child to talk, tend to have the most communicative children.

If you are unsure about whether you are talking to your child in the most effective way, record yourself at key moments of the day and take a critical listen afterwards. Ask yourself the following:

- Did you talk so much that your child didn't have a chance to reply or make noises back to you?
- Was your talk appropriate for the age of your child – not too complicated for little ones but not too simple for older children?
- Were you constantly being interrupted by your partner/older children/telephone?
- Could you hear a lot of background noise such as the TV or radio?
- Did you sound interesting and enthusiastic about what you were saying?
- Did you respond to your child's interruptions?

- Did you sound interested in what your child was saying or excited about the noises she was making?
- Did your child learn anything during the day from what you were saying to her?

3 The physical factor

Hearing loss

The most obvious physical reason why your child might be slower to start talking is poor hearing. This should be checked by health visitors at around eight months but any concerned parents can ask for a check before this. Profoundly deaf children are usually spotted fairly early on. It may be that they seem surprised when their parents suddenly appear at the side of the cot, even after all the usual noises of entering the room; or perhaps they fail to startle in response to a sudden noise or do not become still in response to a more continuous noise.

Some children have more intermittent or fluctuating hearing loss, not hearing properly when they have a bad cold or an ear infection. Middle ear infections, such as glue ear, which cause this occasional hearing loss can be treated easily with antibiotics or grommets (these are inserted into the ear to drain the fluid out). Even this temporary deafness can have an adverse effect on speech and language development. If we have difficulty hearing with a bad cold, we can ask people to speak up or make good guesses at what is being said. A child, however, may not realise that he is missing out on hearing sounds or whole words, and slow speech development can follow. Once treated, children can generally catch up easily although it helps if parents put an extra emphasis on language – playing games, looking at books and talking together.

Cleft palate

Physical problems with the mouth and tongue will obviously affect the sounds of speech, and speech therapy may be needed. Some children may be born with a particular deformity such as a cleft palate. However, operations are so successful now that very often difficulties with speech are minimal. Advice will be given soon after the child is born and a first operation is usually carried out well before the child's first birthday.

A note on feeding problems

Feeding – learning to suck and swallow and then chew – is important for speech development. A chewing action involves moving and exercising the parts of the mouth needed to form sounds and is therefore an important skill to acquire. Interestingly, children usually start to use a more mature chewing pattern at about six to eight months, round about the time when they move on from cooing (open vowel sounds such as 'ooh' and 'aah') to babbling (a greater repertoire of sounds such as 'gaga' and 'baba'). Children who have difficulties with the mechanics of feeding often go on to have problems with speech, which is why speech and language therapists are also experts in feeding patterns.

4 Position in the family

If you have more than one child, you may notice differences between older and younger children. Of course, it's difficult to make too many sweeping generalisations when there are so many other factors to take into account, such as the personality and sex of the child, but even so, there do seem to be certain characteristics common to eldest, middle and youngest children. Amongst other things, communication skills seem to vary according to a child's position in the family and the following generalisations can be made. But remember, they are only generalisations.

Eldest children

Eldest children tend to reach their milestones earlier than younger children and this includes talking. There would seem to be several reasons for this. Of course, with just one child to look after, parents are able to give her more time and will consequently talk more to her, look at more books with her and play more games with her. Parents also admit that they are more likely to try and 'push' older children on and are competitive with other families. Somehow, once you've got one child talking well, it is easy to let number two go at his own leisurely speed – you will be more confident that he will talk eventually, so what's the hurry? Eldest children, particularly where there is quite a large gap before the next child, become very adept and confident at talking with adults. In fact, they may be better at communicating with adults than with their peers. Their competitive nature may mean more disputes with friends and siblings.

Only children

Only children are also more likely talk early for the same reason as eldest children. They may share a lot of adult experiences quite early on, such as being taken to a restaurant, and they are often taken on a wide variety of trips and outings. This may account for why they often have a very good vocabulary. They are also good at communicating with adults – in fact, they tend to consult adults frequently and this may include 'telling tales'.

Middle children

Middle children often receive the least adult attention, particularly where the children are close in age. They therefore progress at their own pace but tend to be slower at talking than older children. They will spend more time communicating with other children than with adults and later on, rarely confide in their parents or discuss problems with them.

Youngest children

Youngest children can be slower at talking, but this depends on the ages of the brothers and sisters. Some are entertained and talked to by both siblings and parents and can consequently learn to talk fairly early. On the other hand, it is common for everybody else in the family to 'baby' the youngest, anticipating her every need so that she doesn't have to talk, and even answering for her. A youngest child may also enjoy being the baby and will therefore be reluctant to grow up – resulting in immature sounding speech. This may be fully accepted by the rest of the family, and where an eldest child may never have said 'doggie' and 'gee-gee', parents may suddenly find this rather cute in the youngest. Typically, the last child in the family has a good sense of humour.

5 Sex differences

Girls generally talk earlier than boys, but boys catch up and by the age of three the differences are very slight. It is unlikely that parents talk more to girls than to boys, so perhaps the edge that girls have is there from birth. Certainly as children get older, the difference becomes more marked as girls continue to be better at using language to work things out and at communicating socially. Many people believe that adult women are better communicators than men and there is certainly evidence to support this. And whatever their ability, it does seem that females like talking more than males do.

Girls tend to use their language ability more to make friends and to socialise. It's not that boys don't want to socialise, they just don't need to talk so much to do so. Just listen to a group of girls playing together and you will hear them chattering away, deciding whether they will pretend to be space monsters or not and planning out who is going to do what. Boys will just *be* space monsters and nothing more need be said.

Girls certainly tend to be earlier in acquiring the sounds of speech and there are more boys than girls referred for speech therapy for difficulty with sounds or for a delay in starting to talk. There are also many more male stammerers than female.

6 Listening and paying attention

Children who are able to give you their full attention when you talk to them, who can spend hours looking at books with you and who listen to every word you say are obviously going to have a head start when it comes to learning to talk. Other children may flit from toy to toy, may crawl off your knee after only one page of their favourite story and may never seem to pay any attention to you whatsoever. Of course, no child gives his undivided attention all the time and you may find that one day your child seems to have very good concentration skills and the next day he's rushing about not listening to anybody or paying attention to anything. Before you jump to the conclusion that your child is a poor listener, it is important to note that attention develops and changes with maturity.

How attention develops

How long a child will concentrate for depends on the situation, her mood and what she is being expected to concentrate on. Nevertheless, there is a general pattern of development which varies little from child to child. Some children will move on to the next stage more quickly than others, so the age guides are only very approximate. (Stages are based on the work of Cooper, Moodley and Reynell, 1978.)

Birth to one – the extremely distractible age At this stage, your baby's attention will be held by the main stimulus at that moment – the toy immediately in front of him, the loud noise of someone entering the room, the rattle just placed into his hand. Then, when something else happens such as a new noise of another toy coming into view, his attention switches to the new item. Your baby may therefore concentrate for quite a long time on one thing but if there are a lot of distractions, he will flit from one thing to another. This emphasises the need for a quiet time to talk to your baby, free from other noises or activity.

DIFFICULTIES AND DIFFERENCES

One to two years – the age of rigid concentration   Your child will be able to concentrate well on a task she enjoys, often so well that it is impossible to distract her from it. She can only cope with one thing at a time, so if you speak to her while she is totally immersed in an activity, she probably won't listen to you at all and you'll be left wondering whether she can hear you. Once you have drawn her attention away, it will then be difficult for her to go back to her activity. This rigid attention can make your child seem very obstinate. During this stage you will therefore need to get your child's undivided attention before you speak to her and then she should listen well. You won't be able to give her instructions about anything while she is actually doing it. She will need to stop first and then listen.

Two to three years – the age of more flexible attention   Your child will be able to switch his attention from his activity to you and then back to the activity again with a little help. He can therefore follow your instructions more readily and has a great capacity for learning at this stage. He won't yet be able to listen to you talking *and* concentrate on his activity at the same time, but he will show a greater ability to stop what he's doing and listen. You may then need to help him redirect his attention back to the task in hand. He will be able to concentrate for slightly longer periods now, so story books become very popular indeed. In fact, you may find yourself reading the same one over and over again!

Three to four years – the age of controlled attention   Your child will be more able to switch her attention from one task to another or from listening to you back to a game or activity. She will rarely flit from toy to toy but will become absorbed in long stretches of meaningful play, concentrating for much longer on activities that interest her. And if what you are talking about interests her, then she will concentrate well on what you are saying.

Four to six years – the age for concentrating at school   To learn at school, children need to concentrate on more than one thing at a time. They need to be able to listen to and take note of what their teacher is saying while they continue with what they are doing. They also need to be able to sustain their concentration for longer periods. This change happens soon after starting school. Of course, some children listen and concentrate better than others and even if your child listens well, there will be times when you may find yourself shouting 'You're not listening to a word I'm saying!' But then you might feel like shouting this to the occasional adult from time to time.

Help your child to listen and concentrate

Good listening skills will help your child to learn and are the key to good language development, but even school children often have problems with listening. This exchange between two seven-year-olds seems to be a good conversation, but Peter hasn't really listened:

Hamish: I go to Sunday school – you should come, it's quite good, Sunday school.
Peter: Yea, but what do you do?
Hamish: Well on Sundays, you go in the hall and you have stories, do pictures and act things out. Sometimes the Sunday school goes in the church.
Peter: Can anyone go?
Hamish: Yea, do you want to come?
Peter: Well I'll give it a try, what day is it on?

Try the following to help your child:

- Don't expect too much. All children need some time to just run around the garden or to day-dream.
- Cut down extra noise in the background when you want your child to concentrate – whether it's on a puzzle, or on what you're saying.
- If your child is easily distracted, remove the distractions, just leaving the activity you want your child to concentrate on.

DIFFICULTIES AND DIFFERENCES

Your child may be able to finish a puzzle better if it's on a bare kitchen table rather than on a bedroom floor full of other toys. She may look at a book and listen to the story for longer if the new puppy is shut in the kitchen for a while.

- Encourage your child to complete a task before starting a new one; perhaps even reward him for doing so. If this is difficult for your child, choose quicker or easier tasks to start with such as a more simple puzzle or a smaller picture to colour in. If he gives up half-way through a book, choose a shorter or easier one to read and talk about.

- If her attention span seems short, time how long your child concentrates for at any one time and then *very* gradually encourage her to concentrate for a little longer.

- Remember that your child needs frequent changes of activity, even though he needs to concentrate for long enough to learn from and enjoy an activity. Don't expect your pre-school child to listen to you talking about books indefinitely. Intersperse talking sessions with some more non-verbal activities. Let your child have some quiet times with no chat at all – thinking time!

- Have a quiet time at least once a day. (Not easy with a large family, but not impossible!)

- Choose an appropriate time of day for carrying out activities which require a lot of concentration or listening. Don't, for example, start reading your youngest child a long story just as the older children are arriving home from school.

- To help your child listen and concentrate while you speak to her, start with her name and maintain eye contact while you talk. If your child never seems to listen, make sure that you give instructions in clear, short sentences.

- Remember that listening skills improve with age. Pre-schoolers will have difficulty in concentrating at least some of the time. There is often a marked improvement between the ages of five and seven.

- Don't expect your child to concentrate for very long on more difficult activities. Likewise, don't expect your child to listen for

very long if the instructions (or the story) are very complicated.
- All children concentrate for longer on activities which they enjoy, and listen harder to something that interests them. (The same goes for adults!) If your child suddenly 'switches off', it may simply be out of boredom!

7 Personality

You will start to get an idea as to what your child's personality is going to be like in the first few months of life. There is no doubt that we are born with many of our characteristics, although at the same time what happens to us during our childhood will inevitably have some effect on personal attributes. Some children will therefore be more shy or more outgoing than others simply because of who they are and the personality they were born with. Whatever her ability, you may simply have a very chatty child or else a child who is reluctant to talk to anyone outside the family. Personality doesn't normally affect the ability to talk that much, but it will affect the way a child uses the language she has. You know you wouldn't swop your child for any other so accept her as she is whether she's driving you mad with her incessant talking or leaving you in despair with her reluctance to talk to anyone other than you. However, confidence in communicating will stand all children in good stead, so make sure your child knows that you find what she tells you interesting and praise her when she talks confidently, especially to people outside the home.

8 Intelligence

A bright, able child is often good at communicating, just as he is good at a number of other things. But a child who is slow to talk is not necessarily less intelligent – just different. Of course, in some cases very poor language development can mean that a child has learning difficulties but all the other areas of his development would need to be investigated thoroughly before this would be clear. Difficulty with talking is not, on its own, an indication of learning difficulties or a low IQ. If a child has delayed speech and language and the therapist notices difficulty with other things, or if a child has been especially slow at reaching all his milestones (sitting, walking, first words, toilet training etc.), then further investigation of the child's general ability may be needed. But there are many bright, able children with speech and language problems who just have speech and language problems, and nothing else.

9 Other experiences

The experiences that a child has in her early years can certainly affect her speech and language development. A child who sits at home all day playing contentedly on her own is at a disadvantage compared with a child who goes out on trips with a parent and is given the opportunity to talk about it all. A child who looks at books with an adult is likely to do better than a child left to browse through one or two on her own. And a child who enjoys going to a nursery or playgroup will also benefit. Children who are left in day nurseries or with a childminder while the parents go to work are not automatically at a disadvantage as far as language development is concerned. If the childminder or nursery staff are not very good at their job, then it is conceivable that a child could be slower to talk than if she had been left at home with mum or dad. However, good care-takers should be every bit as capable as a parent at talking and listening to children; in fact, young children do seem to gain a lot from having a variety of people to relate to and to talk with. They also benefit from the need to communicate with other children and often tend to start school as very social, chatty and confident children.

Another experience of childhood is television. Long hours spent looking at TV programmes will not do much to help a child who is learning to talk. However, watching suitable programmes with a parent can be a very valuable experience indeed.

CHAPTER TEN

Reading, playing, learning and remembering

If you think about it, language – the ability to talk, understand and think in words – is the key to so many other things. We use words to solve problems, to learn, to help us remember things, and we can translate those spoken words into writing. Once a child can start to talk, she can suddenly do so many other things and as her level of understanding increases, so does her capacity to learn.

Language as a pre-reading skill

There are many books which claim that you can teach your baby to read, that you can train your child to see that the shape of the word 'Daddy' actually says 'Daddy' which looks different from the word shape for 'baby'. There may be some success with these methods but there is no point teaching a child to recognise a word he cannot understand or possibly even say. And if your child is just using single words, then even if it were possible to teach him to read, all he could do would be to read a list of words which is neither rewarding nor enjoyable.

Your child needs to know that a sheep is a sheep before he can have any idea that the word written underneath the picture of the woolly animal says 'sheep'. He also needs to be using all the little words that occur in sentences – 'the', 'of', 'to' etc. – before he is able to read them. In other words, your child needs to understand what he is reading for it to have any value at all, and it helps if the words he reads are part of his everyday vocabulary. Obviously, in order to read, your child needs to develop visual skills as well as to reach a certain level of language. Like spoken words, written words are symbols which represent ideas or objects. Pictures are also symbols and your child needs to enjoy looking at pictures in books before she will even notice the words underneath, let alone realise that they mean anything.

Talking as a pre-reading skill

- Introduce your child to books as soon as she shows an interest. Very young babies (under 6 months) will not understand the pictures but may enjoy looking at them just the same. Nine or 10 months is the ideal time for talking about the pictures together. Use board books or plastic books to start with so that your child can play with them on her own as well as look at them with you. She will copy the way you turn the pages over and when you watch her you will notice that she has learnt something already – books start at the front and end at the back.

- Let your toddler help you make your own book using photographs of friends and family. As you stick in each picture, let your child watch you write the name of each person underneath and run your finger under the word as you say it. Still concentrate on talking about the pictures but if in the process she learns that words actually mean something, then she has made a step towards reading.

- Make sure that the books you choose reflect the language level of your child. If, for example, your child is beginning to put words together then she has moved on from needing picture books which feature pictures of everyday objects and will now enjoy pictures of children or animals *doing* things. These generally have more complex pictures full of activity which you can talk about. Once your child is talking about the past and putting ideas together into sentences, she will enjoy simple story books.

- Talk about reading and writing as it occurs. For example, you might draw your child's attention to signposts and notices while you are out and about.
- Before he even starts to read, your child can learn that writing runs from left to right and from the top to the bottom of the page. Run your finger along the words as you read them and you will soon notice your child imitating your actions.
- Once your child is an able reader, she will learn new words from the books which she reads. While she is learning to read, however, it is less confusing if she knows the meaning of words first. Help build up her vocabulary by talking about new things and giving your child new experiences. This will indirectly help her with reading.
- Carry on reading to your child even though he has started to read himself.

How language helps memory

Children are remembering things all the time – it is part of learning. After all, learning a new word involves remembering it so that it can be used again and again.

It is very rare for us to remember anything about our lives before the age when we start to talk. Most people's earliest memories are of when they were two or three, just after they started to talk. But we probably don't need language to remember things and many of our memories will be visual. Nevertheless, language and memory are very closely linked and we have a sort of inner language to store and retrieve our memories. Inner language and thinking are similar. If you just stop and say what you are thinking at any moment, you will probably find it easy to put those thoughts into words. Not all thinking is done in words – after all, children think before they have words – but once we have language, a lot is. In fact, language seems to have quite an affect on our thoughts and understanding. Memory, thinking, language and understanding are therefore all closely linked in the process of learning.

Helping your child to remember language

- Encourage your child to join in with the repetitive lines of favourite stories – 'I'll huff and I'll puff and I'll blow your house down' or 'Run, run as fast as you can, you can't catch me I'm the gingerbread man.' If a story doesn't seem to have a repetitive line in it, then make one up. You don't have to stick to the 'script'.

- Rhymes and rhythm make words and sentences easier to remember. You may notice your child remembering whole lines of nursery rhymes when he's only just beginning to put words together. Sing songs, recite nursery rhymes and make up your own rhythmic songs and poems as you go about your daily routine. You can always adapt nursery rhymes – 'This is the way we have a bath, have a bath, have a bath before we read our story' (to the tune of 'Here we go round the Mulberry Bush'). Or 'Little Jamie put on his socks, Little Jamie put on his shoes' etc. (spoken to the rhythm of 'Humpty Dumpty').

- When your child first starts to talk about recent past events she will find it difficult to recall everything; or she may recall something perfectly well but have difficulty finding the right words, so give her plenty of 'memory joggers'. If, for example, she mentions a trip to the beach the day before, don't just ask endless questions to get her to regurgitate the day's events. Instead, try to remember it together. You might say something like 'We had ice-cream . . . or was it a lolly?' or 'I can't remember what we had for lunch, now let's see . . .'

- Repetition is the key. You will soon notice that your child enjoys listening to the same story or watching the same video over and over again. So why shouldn't he enjoy a certain amount of repetition in your conversations together. You won't bore your child by reinforcing new words and repeating new ideas until you are sure that he has listened, understood and remembered.

• Memory falls into two categories, visual memory and auditory (or listening) memory. There are games to help both, including: Pairs and Kim's game (putting out items on a tray, then removing one) for visual memory to 'I went to market and bought . . .' or a long version of Old Macdonald (with all the animals you can remember) for auditory memory.

• Give your child messages to take to Grandpa in the next room, or the people next door. Make them as long and complicated as your child can cope with.

Language and play

Your child will play long before he is talking, but once he does talk, his play will seem to reach a whole new dimension. He will talk to himself as he plays, verbalising his actions and even having one-way conversations with teddy. Later, he will seem to make decisions out loud as he tells himself what he's going to do next. Once he reaches the stage of playing with other children, he will even discuss the play activity with them and make plans together. Later still, he will make up rules and regulations as he invents new games and activities, and language is then an integral part of playing.

Play is, in many ways, an essential part of learning to talk. Children need to understand that toys can represent real objects as well as learn that words can represent objects. Playing with large dolls, brushing their hair, putting them to bed etc., is therefore important in developing both play and language. Later on, language and play become imaginative and inventive. By the age of three, children will act out stories and events using dolls or play people. They will even invent people and something like a cardboard box can become absolutely anything they can think of. They will

READING, PLAYING, LEARNING AND REMEMBERING

invariably verbalise all this imagination and by age four or five will be making up stories and, at times, living in a world of complete fantasy.

Games for talking

- Let your child take the lead in imaginative games – your role is to join in and have fun, rather than to take over the ideas and inventions.

- If your child gets stuck in the same imaginative game, day after day, the language needed will also be monotonous and repetitive. In this case, you could try to extend the activity by bringing in some new 'props' to spark off new thoughts or, if necessary, start off a new idea yourself. But let your child take over the idea as soon as possible.

- Use everyday incidences to start off a bit of spontaneous play. For example, if someone falls over, you could turn it into a game of doctors or you could cheer up hair-washing time by creating a game of hairdressers.

- Incorporating imaginative games into everyday chores can work wonders. Children are more likely to make their beds in a game of chambermaids or clear the table in a game of waiters and waitresses.

- Don't impose your views on what a particular toy is for. If your child has decided that the toy box is a boat and the skittles are oars, then stick with this rather than trying to think of something better and *never* start saying 'But this isn't what you do with skittles' and start showing him the rules of the game. Just encourage your child to talk about boats as you play and discuss problems such as what to do if the boat sinks.

- Encourage your child to 'act out' his experiences. This will help him to remember them and learn from them. For example, if you have just been to the doctor, you could play at surgeries, incorporating names of body parts and doctor's instruments as well as more complex discussions along the lines of 'What would happen if you spilt your medicine/ate food that had gone off?' or 'What happens when the doctor is ill?'

- Let your child have plenty of opportunity to play and talk on her own. If she is happily chatting as she plays with her doll's house and is working out where she can put the people, then she is enjoying herself, learning, pretending and experimenting with her language skills. What more does she need? So leave well alone.

Toys for talking

Birth to one year
Board and plastic books.
Large dolls and teddies and objects which the child can relate them to, such as a comb, cup and toothbrush.
Mobiles of recognisable objects or pictures.
Telephone.
Baby mirror.
Saucepans and spoons.

One to two years
Books.
Duplo bricks (or similar) with Duplo people.
Wooden bricks.
Tea set.
Playdough and cooking utensils.
Sandpit with cars and lorries.
Bowl of water with boats and people.
Crayons and paper.
Wendy house (can be made out of two chairs and a sheet).

Two to three years
Books.
Farm set.
Play people.
Dressing up clothes (your old cast-offs are perfect).

READING, PLAYING, LEARNING AND REMEMBERING

Picture lotto.
Song tapes and musical instruments (home-made drums and shakers are ideal).
Fuzzy-felt board games (make your own – felt sticks to felt).
Glove puppets (made from old socks) or finger puppets (a face drawn on to a finger will do).

Three to four years
Books.
Picture pairs.
Picture dominoes.
Story tapes.
Play people.
Shop (a collection of empty packets and cartons and plastic money).
Floor-mat layout (buy or make a layout of a town with streets).

Four to five years
Books.
Simple board games.
Many of the items previously mentioned, particularly play people.
Ambiguous items which can be used as anything in an imaginative game, for example, cardboard boxes, old clothes, the table covered in a blanket etc.

Five to ten years
Books.
Board games with varying rules.
Recommended games such as: 'Twister' (MB Games); 'Guess Who?' (MB Games); 'Whatever Next?' (Living and Learning); various quiz games.
Computer games to play with a friend, or pencil or paper games.

Language and learning

When we learn something, we invariably do it with the aid of words. We read words in books, listen to words on the television or listen to someone explaining something new to us. Children also learn through words but a lot of their learning is done without words – from discovering that the ball that rolled behind the couch is still there to finding out how to get the right balance to ride a bicycle. Of course, words can help in some of these situations and an explanation of which foot to put on the peddles first goes hand-in-hand with the trial and error tactics children use when attempting their first bike ride. Children gradually learn language and at the same time, they are using that language to learn about other things.

Talking as an aid to learning

- Your child needs to hear her own voice as well as yours. It reinforces her language skills and helps her to tackle difficult tasks by 'talking them through'. If your child is playing and talking, don't automatically intervene. Let her think, talk and learn her way through.
- Your child doesn't need to be taught, he needs to learn. In other words, don't just teach him, say, the words for size such as 'big' and 'little', but let him experience them by playing with and matching big and little items. Just gently feed in the words 'big', 'little', 'biggest' etc. when he is ready.
- Some activities require a lot of talking from you – looking at books and so on. But talking can intervene with learning in certain situations. For example, if your two-year-old is experimenting with trying to fit different sized beakers into each other, she needs to experiment and to think. A lot of talking, by way of explanations from you, can stop her from working it out for herself. In this type of situation, you might be better to give her some non-verbal help if she gets frustrated, or leave her to learn on her own. Language can help, but wait before you talk. If she has worked out a task for herself, *then* praise her and talk about what she's done.
- There is more to learning new concepts than knowing the words. For example, children can easily pick up the names of

READING, PLAYING, LEARNING AND REMEMBERING

colours but they haven't really learnt about colours until they can match the right word to the right colour. Non-verbal tasks such as matching colours must be learnt well before naming them, so give your child the opportunity to look at colours first – perhaps drawing her attention to them by threading all the blue beads on to one string and all the red ones on to another string. There are many words that your child might use before fully understanding them and numbers come into this category. In these instances, the words are in many ways less important than the underlying meaning.

- Learning and language are all about opportunity and experiences. But how do you give your child the right experience? Observe your child carefully and you will see if he is learning from his play. Listen to the conversations you have with him and you can get a feel for what he is getting out of your words.

Parent traps

Look out for the following parent traps:

- Too much stimulation. Are there so many stimulating toys around that your child doesn't know which way to turn?
- Too much talking from you. Does your child have time to think? Learning needs a lot of 'inner digestion', so give your child a chance to take in what you say.
- Do you intervene too much or too little? Knowing just when to butt into a child's activity with a suggestion or helpful comment is a difficult skill.

Language is a tool that helps us to do other things, from thinking to making a friend. Interestingly the particular language we use, in our case English, can have an effect on what we learn and think. Eskimos, for example, have several different words for snow and very young children learning these words also learn to see the differences between the different types of snow. In English, we only have one word for snow and therefore don't look for the differences in the type of snow that has fallen. It was only in the winter of 1990 when British Rail had problems with clearing a particular type of snow that we even noticed that, indeed, it was a softer, finer snow than previous years. So although different types of snow fall in this country, we don't have the language to describe them so exactly and therefore we don't have such an easy way of identifying them.

Now consider the way your child learns. If she doesn't have, say, the words for all the different types of animals then she may not seem to notice the differences – all four-legged animals are dogs to her. But give her the language, hand-in-hand with the experience, and she will quickly learn. In fact, during the years of learning to talk, your child's knowledge and ability to learn will seem to progress almost daily – you won't be able to keep up with everything she is learning!

CHAPTER ELEVEN

Speech therapy

What is a speech and language therapist?

Speech and language therapists used to be called speech therapists and still are in some parts of the country – they are one and the same. They simply changed their name so that the general public would, hopefully, be more aware that their role is more than dealing with speech (articulation) problems.

Speech and language therapists work with adults – those who've had a stroke, have a stammer, have lost their voice or who are mentally handicapped – as well as with children of all ages who have feeding or communication problems. They help children who are slow to talk, who have difficulty expressing themselves or who have problems understanding what others are saying in a way which is not appropriate for their age. They treat children who have diffi-culty with the sounds of speech, who are non-fluent (stammer) who have hoarse voices or who have a physical deformity such as a cleft palate. They work with the deaf, the mentally handicapped and the physically handicapped. In other words, speech and language therapists deal with communication problems of any sort, working in health clinics, hospitals and schools. They also have a particular interest in preventing any problems and educating the public about normal speech and language development. They give talks, provide leaflets and visit playgroups to ensure that parents are aware of what language skills can be expected from each age group and of what their roles are in helping their child to communicate well.

What speech and language therapists *don't* do

They are not elocutionists. They do not wish to change anybody's accent or dialect. They do not treat children who use slang, drop their *h*s or mumble by choice.

When to see the speech and language therapist

If you are at all concerned about your child's talking, then you should ask your health visitor or GP for a referral to a speech and language therapist. Here are some rough guidelines:

- If your child reaches the age of two and has no words and is not using jargon (jargon is the name for long strings of babble which are uttered with the intonation, or up and down pattern, of normal speech).
- If your child is two-and-a-half and has less than a dozen words and is not putting words together.
- If your child is three and uses very few phrases (short sentences).
- If your child is three and you have difficulty understanding what she is saying.
- If your child is three-and-a-half and cannot be understood by strangers at all, even if *you* know what he's saying.
- If your child is five or more and has very hesitant speech.
- If your child has difficulty with a particular sound and, on consulting the chart opposite, you find she should have been using this sound six months previously.

- If your child has a hoarse or nasal-sounding voice and has had a full ear, nose and throat examination first.
- If you have *any* worries concerning your child's speech and language development whatever his or her age.

Rough guide to when your child will start using speech sounds

p, b, t, d, n, m – by age two.
w, s, f, v, z – by age three.
g, k – by age three-and-a-half.
l, y and sound blends such as *st, sm, sn* etc. – by age four.
ch, j, sh – usually by age four to four-and-a-half.
th, r – usually by age six.

How to see a speech and language therapist

In some areas a referral directly from a parent is acceptable. In other words, telephone your local health clinic (listed under your health authority in the telephone directory), ask for the speech and language therapist and then make an appointment. However, a referral from another professional is preferable and in most areas necessary, so ask your health visitor, GP or your child's teacher to refer your child for speech therapy. If your health visitor is reluctant to refer your child but you are nevertheless concerned, be insistent. If absolutely necessary, telephone the speech therapy department yourself and explain the situation. They will be very sympathetic.

Sometimes your health visitor may suggest speech therapy to your complete surprise. Perhaps you were unaware that there was any problem. Do agree to go along. If there isn't a problem then the speech and language therapist will tell you or else it may be a matter of giving you some advice and keeping a check on your child's progress rather than attending regular sessions. There should be no stigma attached to speech therapy – many otherwise bright and healthy children see a speech and language therapist and generally enjoy the sessions.

What the speech and language therapist will do

Most children enjoy going to see the speech and language therapist. Her (or his) room is not usually like a doctor's surgery but is more like a playroom. Your child may play games or look at pictures and will certainly be given plenty of time to settle in and feel at home. If you are very worried about the visit your child may pick up your anxiety and become nervous herself, so try to relax and encourage your child to look forward to going to see some new toys.

On the first visit, the therapist will spend quite a lot of time talking to you. She will want to discuss your view of the problem as well as take details of your child's development. She will also chat and play with your child and may even carry out a more formal assessment. Even the assessments are enjoyed by many children, who probably won't realise that they are being 'tested'. The tests usually consist of looking at specific toys and pictures and either following simple instructions or talking about the items. The therapist will then discuss the problem with you, as she sees it, and make some suggestions about what course of action to take. In some cases, she may suggest referring your child to another specialist. This could include an ear, nose and throat consultant or an educational psychologist, or she may advise that your child has her hearing checked. She will then tell you what, if any, speech therapy your child needs. This may involve coming to the clinic every week or just occasionally for a check-up. It may involve attending a group or having one-to-one therapy. In either case, the therapist will give you a rough guide as to how long treatment is likely to last.

You will be given advice about how to deal with the problem at home and will be expected to carry out specific activities between appointments. In fact, speech therapy very much consists of cooperation between the parents, the therapist and the child. You will be expected to work with your child following the guidelines

SPEECH THERAPY

set out by the therapist and in many instances, the sessions will be largely used to initiate a programme for you to carry out at home.

How to get the best out of your speech and language therapist

- Attend sessions regularly and always telephone if you cannot make one.
- Listen carefully to the suggestions made by the therapist. Always remember that she is trying to help you and your child. Don't misinterpret this as a criticism of you as a parent.
- Ask your therapist to give you a rough idea of how long treatment is likely to take. After a few sessions, ask her how she thinks your child is progressing.
- Watch what the therapist does carefully as you will probably be asked to practise the activities at home. If you are not invited to sit in on the sessions, ask why.
- Try not to take brothers and sisters along with you, particularly if they are likely to distract the child having therapy. Ask a friend or neighbour if they can help out.
- Make sure that you are absolutely clear about what the therapist wants you to do at home. Report back to her next time on how you got on. If your child disliked an activity or found it too difficult, tell the therapist. She relies on your feedback.
- If you have specific tasks to carry out, make sure that you choose a quiet time when your child seems to be in a cooperative mood. Do a little each day – don't forget about it all week and then cram it all into the hour before your appointment.
- Do ask your therapist if there are any toys or books which you could buy to help your child. Join the library if you haven't already done so, and ask the therapist if there is a toy library in your area.
- Always ask your therapist if you don't understand anything. They often have their own jargon and it is easy for them to slip into it without realising.

- If you are not satisfied with your therapist or feel your child has a very poor relationship with her, then ask to speak to the head of the department (speech therapy manager, area/district speech therapist or chief speech therapist). It may be possible to receive treatment from a different therapist.
- If your child is put on to a waiting list, ask what you can do to help your child in the meantime.
- Your child may be seen in a group with other children. Don't think this means she is getting less therapy. Many children respond better to the more natural communication setting a group provides. Ask your therapist to explain her reasons for putting your child into a group.
- Your child may be seen at school. Ask if you can attend the sessions.

At a glance guide to speech and language problems

Delayed language development This describes a child whose level of talking and understanding would be more appropriate to a younger child. Sometimes a child can understand at an appropriate level for his age but his sentence structure and vocabulary are delayed.

Delayed speech development This describes a child whose use of speech sounds would be more appropriate to a younger child. For example, a four-year-old who still says 'tat' for 'cat' would have delayed speech (or phonology). Children with delayed language development will often have delayed speech as well because language and speech normally develop alongside each other.

Deviant speech Sometimes the speech sounds used by a child are not typical of a younger child and are not part of normal adult speech. A lisp would come into this category.

Specific language disorder This is sometimes a more long-term problem and can be regarded as something a child may have been born with. More intensive speech therapy is needed, perhaps in a language unit attached to a primary school. The aim of a language unit is to give each child speech therapy and teaching with a specific emphasis on language. Hopefully the children can be gradually integrated back into the normal classroom.

Stammering (stuttering is simply the American word for this). Young children who have hesitant speech, repeating sounds and words in a fairly easy manner are not usually called stammerers. They are described as non-fluent and have a good chance of growing out of this phase. However, a very small percentage do go on to be teenage and adult stammerers. These people are very aware of their problem, their communication skills are affected and in some cases there is an effect on personality. There is no known cause for stammering, although there are many theories. Many people believe it is a disorder you are born with and there is an hereditary factor.

Voice disorders   Hoarse voices, very nasal or breathy voices or a delay in a boy's voice breaking may all be problems looked at by a speech and language therapist. These children will already have been seen by the ear, nose and throat (ENT) specialist and may be treated in that department. The speech and language therapist is particularly interested in children who don't use their voices properly (perhaps they force their voice when they sing or shout) and children who need therapy following surgery.

Cleft palate   A physical deformity present at birth. The child may also have a cleft lip. Normally the soft palate (the back part of the roof of the mouth) can open and close and will be closed for most sounds of speech so that air does not escape through the nose during speech. With a cleft palate, the palate, or roof of the mouth, has a hole in it so that air can run freely between the nose area and the mouth. Surgery is very effective and is generally carried out when the child is still a baby. Following surgery, a child may need speech therapy to help the palate move effectively.

Some children without cleft palates as such have an **incompetent**

soft palate (one that doesn't close well or at the right time). This may not require surgery but may need exercises to stop speech being too nasal.

Other words you may hear

Phonology   Refers to articulation or the sounds of speech.

Aphasia   A specific language disorder. An aphasic child may be of normal intelligence but has difficulty making sense of language and expressing herself.

Autistic   A particular handicap which will include difficulty with language. Typically, an autistic child may use long sentences of learnt speech – set phrases which have been remembered but not necessarily understood.

Syntax   Another word for grammar or sentence structure.

Elective mute   A child who can talk well but has decided not to communicate either all the time or in set situations, such as at school.

Vocal cord nodules   These will cause voice problems and may be the result of recurrent laryngitis or misuse of the voice. They can be cured with voice rest. Surgery is sometimes needed.

Glue ear (secretory otitis media)   Fluid in the middle ear which causes a temporary hearing loss. This is sometimes treated with **Grommets** which are surgically implanted in the ear to create an even pressure between the different sections of the ear.

Tongue-tie   The frenum of the tongue (the bit that joins the tongue to the bottom of the mouth) is very short and impedes tongue movement. Contrary to popular belief, this rarely affects speech, but when it does, there will probably be an associated difficulty with feeding.

Useful addresses

THE COLLEGE OF SPEECH AND LANGUAGE THERAPISTS, 7 Bath Place, Rivington Street, London EC2A 3DR. Tel: 0171 613 3855

THE ASSOCIATION OF ALL SPEECH IMPAIRED CHILDREN (AFASIC), 347 Central Market, Smithfield, London EC1 9NH. Tel: 0171 236 6487

PLAYMATTERS (The Toy Libraries Association), Seabrooks House, Wyllyotts Manor, Darkes Lane, Potters Bar, Hertfordshire EN6 2HL.

ROYAL NATIONAL INSTITUTE FOR THE DEAF (RNID), 105 Gower Street, London WC1E 6AH. Tel: 0171 387 8033

Index

King Alfred's
Winchester

Martial Rose Library
Tel: 01962 827306